Flame

in the

Hollow

Delilah Synn

Trigger Warnings

Graphic Violence

Beheadings

Gore and blood splatter

Sword combat with brutal injuries

Burnings and spectral explosions

Death

Ectoplasmic jizz

On-page character death

Civilian casualties

Sexual Content

Explicit, graphic sexual scenes

Rough sex (consensual, ghostly)

References to past sexual activity in degrading terms

Psychological Trauma

Grief, loss, and betrayal

Madness and obsession

Supernatural Horror

Hauntings

Ghost possession

Spiritual resurrection

War Themes

Betrayal during battle

Flashbacks to military trauma

Cursing / Profanity

Frequent use of strong language

Degradation

Crude references to a woman's body during confrontation

Religious Undertones / Afterlife

Spirits, ghosts, and judgment in death

A character with a split personality

Fire / Burning Deaths

Multiple fiery deaths described in graphic detail

Animal Death

Implied destruction from spectral chaos affecting the environment

Blood Magic

Spirit Tethering

Author's Note

Thank you for mounting up and venturing into the shadows of Flame in the Hollow. This story galloped out of my obsession with the Legend of Sleepy Hollow. I've created a place where the line between justice and vengeance is as thin and fragile as a leaf on a cold autumn night. Here, the Headless Horseman doesn't just haunt the woods; he rides through every page, a restless spirit chasing truth, love, and retribution all at once.

As an avid collector of Headless Horseman statues, I've always been fascinated by that chilling silhouette- the headless torso, the flying cloak, and the Jack-o- lantern. This book is my dark tribute to that legend.

So, are you ready to ride with me at midnight? Hold tight ! The journey through Flame in the Hollow is not for the faint of heart.

With restless spirits and wicked passion,
- Delilah Synn

Playlist

The Apparition - Sleep Token
French Girls - Dove Cameron
BLACK swan SWAN lake - District 78
Bad Decisions - Bad Omens
Mitternacht - E Nomine
My Curse - Killswitch Engage
Love Story - Indila
Devil in Disguise - Marino
Your Betrayal - Bullet for My Valentine
Laid to Rest - Lamb of God
Legends Never Die - Against the Current

Contents

Dedication

This tale is for anyone who believes that beneath every ghost story lurks a heartbeat that can haunt you.

Prologue

Sans Tête

(Headless)

White Plains, 1776

The morning mist clung to the battlefield like a ghost that refused to leave. It crawled between soldiers' legs and soaked into their boots, dampening socks, numbing toes, making them feel like death was grasping at their ankles to drag them to hell.

Brigadier General Adderley sat tall on his blood-flecked horse, eyes sharp and mouth already twisted into a sneer. His red coat flared behind him, spotless and perfect, like he hadn't already walked through a hundred dying men to get here. He surveyed the sea of

British and Hessian soldiers like a god looking down on ants and finally raised his voice, slicing through the fog like a saber.
"Today, we make those rebel bastards choke on their own cocks. We send them running, screaming, bleeding from holes they didn't know they had. We remind them the Crown owns their land, their families, their fucking souls!"

Roars erupted. War cries broke like a dam bursting. Sabers raised. Muskets slammed to shoulders. Bloodlust filled the air.

Adderley dismounted. His boots splashed into mud already dark with piss and old blood. He walked to a soldier waiting at the edge of the formation.

Steffan Weber.

A Hessian, sure. But also a beast on the battlefield. Tall as hell, carved like a statue from a darker age. His black hair was pulled back with an obsidian ribbon, a few wild strands curling around high cheekbones. His uniform was pristine. Too pristine. His eyes were the color of storm clouds and war. He was too perfect to survive this world. But too deadly to belong in the next.

Adderley handed him a folded letter bound with a ribbon redder than fresh meat.

"For your family," he said, voice low. "You're not coming back."

Steffan didn't blink. Just took it, slipped it inside his coat like it was just another letter.

"Germany should be proud of you," Adderley added.
"Hell, I'm proud of you. You'll die, but you'll make it
fucking worth it."

Steffan mounted his black stallion like it was born for
him. Together, they looked like the Devil's shadow had
grown a spine and sharpened its teeth.

Then came the charge.
Everything exploded.
Muskets flared. Cannonballs ripped through the trees.
Soldiers screamed as their insides spilled into the dirt.
Blood sprayed in arcs. Bones cracked like kindling.
There was a wet pop every time a bullet hit something
soft. The air stank of gunpowder, shit, and torn-open
guts.

Steffan rode straight through it like he couldn't be
touched. Like war feared him. He twisted in the saddle,
sword flashing silver through smoke. A rebel's head
came clean off, neck spurting hot red blood as his body
crumpled. He split another man from collarbone to
crotch, innards unspooling like wet, uncased sausages.
Every kill was precise, brutal, and beautiful.

His horse trampled a screaming man under hoof, ribs
crunching like dry leaves. His eyeballs popped onto the
battlefield as hooves crushed his head. Mud and blood
sprayed from the impact. Steffan didn't even glance
down.

He was almost to the hill. Almost to the rebel officer
who hadn't seen him coming. His blade was slick and

dripping. His eyes locked on the target like nothing else mattered.

Then everything shattered.
The first cannonball hit his horse dead in the side. The beast shrieked before collapsing in a spray of bone, blood, and black muscle. Steffan was thrown, smashing into the ground hard enough to knock the wind out of the world.
He rolled, coughing up dirt, head spinning. Blood smeared his cheek. Something in his ribs crunched with every breath.

He blinked, trying to make sense of the sky above him. Then he saw it. The second cannonball. Dark. Spinning. Whistling.
Coming straight for him.
It wasn't from the rebels.

It was from the British. From his side. The fucking Hessians.

He had time to register it. Just enough time for the betrayal to sink in like a blade in the back.

Then darkness.

It didn't just kill him. It obliterated him.

Everything above his shoulders vanished in a spray of meat and heat and bone. Blood splattered the grass ten feet in every direction. Bits of teeth. Chunks of skull. A ribbon fluttered down and landed in the blood soaked mud like a fallen obsidian crown.

They never found his head.

Not the Redcoats. Not the rebels. Not the scavengers
that came after.

But some say, when the wind turns sharp and thunder
grumbles over the Hollow, you can see him riding again.
Headless. Furious. Still soaked in the blood of men who
tried to stop him.

The Headless Horseman was born that day at White
Plains.
And he's still not fucking done.

Chapter 1

Oui, Maîtresse

(Yes, Mistress)

The bell above the schoolhouse rang out like it demanded attention in the same way Odette Fournier did. She opened the door and stepped inside, her high-heeled boots clicked across the worn, creaky, wooden floorboards, each step purposeful and elegant. The scent of chalk, ink, and children lingered in the air like a ghost trapped in the very essence that was the school. The children sat stiffly in their seats, eyes wide as they watched the new headmistress glide toward the front of the classroom.

She turned slowly, hands folded at her waist, her gaze sweeping across the rows of tiny desks.
"Stand," she said. Her voice was calm yet firm.
The children immediately stood.
"Now," she said with a hint of amusement playing at her lips, "Let us begin."

Odette Fournier was thirty years old and possessed a presence that could silence a room with nothing more than her posture. Her golden hair was thick and glossy, always pinned in elegant styles that revealed the curve of her swan-like neck. Her eyes were a pale, icy blue, framed by long, dark lashes that gave them an almost feline quality. Her clothes were always tasteful and feminine, flowing dresses made with soft fabrics that moved with the grace of a beautiful, white swan.

She had been born in New Orleans and educated in Paris. There was something in her voice, a rhythm foreign to the Hudson Valley, and something in her gaze that unsettled the residents of Sleepy Hollow. She walked with the confidence of a woman who could handle anything the world flung her way.

Replacing Ichabod Crane has not been difficult. He had been a peculiar man, stiff like he had the handle of a rake shoved up his ass and nervous like he had never seen his own cock. His sudden disappearance nearly a year ago still hung over the town like a black storm cloud. Some said he fled the town because he couldn't handle the torment of Brom van Brundt and Katrina van Tassel. Others whispered of darker fates. No one said the words aloud, but all thought it.

The Headless Horseman.

The legend clung to the town like ivy scrolling up a trellis. The Headless Horseman, cloaked in black, carrying a fiery jack 'o' lantern, riding through the woods under the cover of night, seeking the head he had lost to a stray cannonball.

Ichabod had ridden his horse into the gaping asshole of demise.

Odette had no patience for ghost stories. She was a woman of letters, of logic. The Horseman was a myth. A tale to frighten children into obedience. Still, she kept a lantern by her bedside. Just in case.

She was quickly making a name for herself in Sleepy Hollow, though not all of it flattering. With her students, she was stern. With the townsfolk, she was witty, sharp, sometimes dismissive. Her mannerisms struck some as arrogant, others as foreign. Yet no one could deny the change she brought. The children were learning again. The schoolhouse had life. Books lined the shelves, maps hung on the walls, and lessons went beyond memorization. Odette taught them to think, to question, to understand the world.

"She is not like Crane," the butcher had said to the baker one morning. Loudly over a pint of mead for all to hear.

"No," the baker had replied. "She's a whore, you can tell. What I wouldn't do to have her spank me and call me 'rascal.'"

"T-thats the name you're going with?!" The butcher laughed, spitting out his mead right on the baker's fresh baguettes.

The baker took a cloth and dabbed the crust, "Well, what would you suggest?"

"For you?" The butcher asked, still hysterically laughing, "Cocksucker."

And yet, they respected her. She gave them reason to. Sleepy Hollow was a curious place. Politically liberal, intellectually cautious, and deeply superstitious. Change was welcome in theory, but often feared in practice. Odette Fournier embodied change. She brought new ideas, spoke her mind, and walked alone through the town without apology.

But as the leaves began to turn into the Autumn versions of themselves, and the nights grew colder, something shifted in the air. A thick mist began to settle over the fields at dawn, refusing to lift even when the sun was high. Dogs barked at nothing. Horses startled at shadows. The forest beyond the schoolhouse felt darker, the trees whispering in a language no one could quite understand.

Odette noticed. She was not a woman to speak of feelings, but she felt it all the same.
She would not be frightened. Not by townsfolk, not by superstition, not by the stories told around fires when the nights stretched into mornings.
Still, she kept her lantern close and locked the door to the schoolhouse every evening with a careful turn of the key.

There were some lessons even a headmistress could not teach.

And some shadows that even she could not quite dismiss.
Late at night, long after the town had become silent and the moon had climbed high above the trees, Odette would sometimes rise from her bed without waking. Her steps would echo softly across the floor as she moved to the mirror in the corner of her room.

She would stare into the glass, her reflection staring back with something unfamiliar in its eyes. A smile that wasn't hers.
A black swan.

In return for a peaceful night she would whisper, "Oui, maîtresse."

Chapter 2

Tu Me Dégoûtes

(You Disgust Me)

A cold and foggy morning broke across the village of Sleepy Hollow. Mist clung to the ground, reluctant to release its grip, curling around fence posts and bare branches of the trees. It was as if the ghosts that had been left behind in the war were clinging to the land. Unwilling to let go. Unable to move on. In the upstairs bedroom of the schoolhouse, Odette sat at her writing desk, a small, pink rose adorned porcelain cup of coffee untouched beside her. Her brow furrowed.

She had forgotten the damn milk.

It was a rare slip in her otherwise impeccable planning. Today, she had intended to bake gâteau de riz, a French rice pudding cake sweetened with cinnamon and lemon peel, for her students. A small cultural indulgence, to elevate their tastes beyond apple tarts and molasses buns. The milk was essential, and the bottle in her pantry was nearly empty.

Shit.

Odette stood, sliding the desk drawer shut with a soft click. She dressed with her usual elegance- a soft ivory blouse, the collar edged in lace, and a rich navy skirt cinched at the waist with a velvet ribbon. Her hair, slightly tousled from restless sleep, was twisted into a loose chignon at the nape of her neck. She applied only a touch of rouge, more for war paint than beauty.
She glanced once at the mirror and paused.

The woman staring back seemed unfamiliar for a breath...eyes too sharp, the curve of the smile too sly. But Odette blinked and the image was her own again.

Milk. Just milk.

The van Brunts would have some for sure.

She grabbed her wicker basket and stepped out into the fog-laced, October morning.

The van Brunt household was one of the larger homes in Sleepy Hollow, built with gray, weathered stone and the blood, sweat and tears of its construction workers it was truly a sight to behold. The winter kissed ivy crawling along its sides almost made it seem like spectral arms were crawling up from hell to tear it down- roof to foundation. A thin line of smoke rose

from the chimney. The garden gate creaked as Odette
let herself in and walked the path to the front door,
lined with late-blooming asters.

She knocked twice.

After a few moments, the door swung open to reveal
Katrina van Brunt, her hair unbound and thick as golden
wheat, her arms full with a sleeping infant nestled
against her breast. The baby's skin was pale and
delicate, a tangle of dark curls peeking beneath her
linen bonnet.

"Odette," Katrina said, breathless. "Forgive the mess. I
wasn't expecting anyone so early."

"I find mornings are more efficient," Odette replied with
a polite smile. Her eyes flicked to the child. "She's
beautiful. What have you named her?"

Katrina smiled, rocking the child gently. "Her name is
Tempest. It came to me the night she was born, just as
the storm struck."

Odette tilted her head. "A bold name."

"She's a bold girl," Katrina said. "She hardly sleeps.
Demands things without apology. I think she'll be the
one to challenge her father."

"Ah." Odette's smile turned dry. "Well that won't be
difficult."

Katrina laughed, and adjusted Tempest slightly in her
arms. "What brings you?"

"I need milk," Odette said, holding up her basket. "For a dessert I intended to make for my students today. I'm afraid I miscalculated how much I had."

"Of course," Katrina said. "Wait here, I'll get some from the kitchen."

She turned and disappeared down the hall.

Odette remained in the doorway. A beam of sunlight caught her face, turning her eyes to silver. She was tracing the grain of the wood on the doorframe with her finger when her concentration was suddenly and irritatingly broken.

"Well, well. Look what the devil dragged in by the pussy."

Odette's lips pursed and she closed her eyes tightly. She did not look up.

Brom van Brunt stepped into view, shirtless beneath his suspenders and his hair a tousled mess of black curls. Odette thought it looked like pubic hair.

There was a smear of dirt on his collarbone and the unmistakable scent of whiskey still lingering on his breath.
"Good morning, Brom," Odette said coldly.

"Morning? With a woman like you on the porch, it's practically Christmas." He grinned, leaning against the doorframe. "You know, if you needed milk, you could've just squeezed it straight from Katrina's tits. Would've made my cock hard. I'd've even warmed it for you."

Odette didn't flinch. Her voice dropped like a blade.

"Tu me dégoûtes."

He blinked, amused. "Don't know what that means, but you make it sound sexy."

"It means you disgust me."

He stepped closer in an attempt to be intimidating. "You know, I've always liked your type. Pretty mouth, sharp tongue. You act like you're too good for this town, but I see the way you look at me. You want someone who can handle you."

She leaned forward just slightly. Her breath was like frost.

"If I ever wanted to feel something repulsive crawl over me, I'd rather wade into the river with the leeches."

His smile faltered and an uglier expression replaced it.

At that moment, Katrina returned with a small glass jug in hand.

"Here you are," she said cheerfully, unaware. "Creamy and fresh from yesterday morning."

Brom chuckled," I'll give you something-"

Odette stepped back, taking the milk with a graceful nod.

"Merci."

"Cum guzzling thunder-cunt," Brom muttered under his breath and disappeared outside to chop wood.

Katrina sighed, watching him go. "Ignore him. He's been worse since Tempest was born. Jealous of the attention."

Odette gave no reply.

"I'm glad you stopped by, truly," Katrina continued. "Everyone in town's grateful for what you're doing. The children needed someone like you. It's been too long since there was a proper instructor. Since Ichabod… well."

Odette raised an eyebrow. "Since he tucked his tail and ran?"

Katrina's expression shifted, more serious now. "That's what some say. I don't believe it, though. Not after what we found."
"What did you find?" Odette asked, lightly tapping her nails against the milk jug.

"His hat and satchel," Katrina said quietly. "Half-buried near the edge of the forest. Scorched like it had been struck by lightning. He's not the first to vanish near there, you know. Others have gone missing over the years. Wanderers. Even a few townsfolk."

Odette gave a dismissive laugh. "Ghost stories. Every backwoods village has them. And Ichabod Crane was a simpering, spineless man who didn't belong here. He probably fled to Boston and took up poetry."

Katrina hesitated. "Maybe. But if you ask me, the Headless Horseman doesn't care about poetry. He cares about trespass."

"You're fucking serious?" Odette asked, arching a brow. "You believe in that tale?"

Katrina looked down at Tempest and smoothed her blanket. "I didn't. Not until the disappearances. Not until that night. I heard the hooves in the woods. Midnight is when he comes. If you're smart, you'll stay away from the forest after dark. Especially then."

Odette's smile was slow and unfazed.

"Don't pique my curiosity," she scoffed. "I might just have some fun with your phantom menace."
Katrina's eyes widened. "Odette, please don't joke about that!"

But the headmistress had already turned, her shawl catching the breeze like a raven wing.

"I have a dessert to prepare," Odette called over her shoulder. "Your milk will go to good use."

She walked back to the schoolhouse, the milk in hand and her thoughts brimming over with interest. A ghost. A legend dressed in death and leather. Foolishness.

Yet...

There was a stirring inside her. A thrill. Not fear, but a hunger for mystery. For control. That stirring made herself known more than Odette liked to admit.
She would bake the gâteau de riz, and serve it with a smile.

Perhaps tonight, she would walk to the edge of the forest.
Just to see if anything answered when she called out.

Chapter 3

L'orgie

(The Orgie)

The gâteau de riz was warm and fragrant, creamy and rich beneath its caramelized top. Odette had spent the morning perfecting it, carefully folding in the vanilla and zest of lemon until it tasted just right. She served it to the children that afternoon, watching their eyes light up as the sweet rice and delicate flavors melted on their tongues. It was a small thing, but it mattered. It was a little piece of France in the hollow of America. A reminder that she had lived and learned in another world, one that she carried with her always.

That night, the taste of the gâteau still lingering on her taste buds, Odette dressed for the van Tassel Fall Soiree. Katrina's father held it every year in the grand old hall of his estate. This wasn't the kind of gathering where people sipped cider and gossiped about their neighbors. It was the kind of party where you needed to fart outside before you went in.

It was an orgy and Odette would never miss it.

She slipped into her favorite dress, a blue silk one that left her shoulders bare and showed off a scandalous amount of cleavage. It made her feel dangerous. She let her hair tumble in loose waves and brushed her lips with a soft rose color that glowed in the candlelight. The night was cool and cruel. It made her nipples hard and she was hungry for it.

She rode her white horse, Perle, to the van Tassel's manor and tied her off to a tree near the forest. Before she even stepped inside, the air had already carried the scent of honeyed wine and the sound of unhinged laughter. She could see the shadows of bodies moving together in the flickering candlelight that backlit the dark windows like a tangled mess of spirits trying to escape the depths of hell. Horny bastards and filthy sluts. Right where she belonged.

At least right where part of her belonged.

Her eyes darkened as she began to walk the gravel path up to the wooden door of the manor. The white swan who was the headmistress of their schoolhouse and taught their children was left outside the moment she crossed the threshold and became the black swan sex goddess that lived for adventure. Especially ones that gave her so many little deaths she didn't think she could return to the land of the unsexed living.

The air inside was heavy with musk and the heat of too many bodies pressed together. Wax dripped slowly onto the floor, shadows of writhing limbs dancing across the walls in sinuous silhouettes. The scent of sex and ass was everywhere, thick and sweet like overripe fruit mingling with sweat. If it was bottled as a perfume it could only be described as something sinful that made her mouth water.

She moved down the hallway, her heels clicking softly on the polished wood, her skirts brushing her bare thighs. She let herself breathe it in, every scent and every flicker of movement. The doorways she passed were half-open, each room a glimpse into another fevered world.

In one room, a man knelt between two women, one hand wrapped around a soft tit, the other gripping its twin on the woman beside her. He moved between them, his slick mouth completely devouring their cunts. Their gasps and cries echoed off the walls each time his fingers clenched, leaving dimples and nail marks blooming on their skin.

In another room, a brunette woman with a sharp smile and a leather harness guided a gruff, hairy behemoth of a man onto his knees, the crack of a whip marking the rhythm of their play. Odette paused, watched the man's head bow, curly black hair shielding his eyes like a curtain. The woman's eyes blazed with power as she took control. She slowly lifted the man's chin and whispered, "Buen chico."

The thought of a man submitting to her like that made Odette instantly wet.

Further down the hall, she saw a red-headed woman with massive, swinging tits wearing a steel strap-on, furiously thrusting into a man's asshole. His skin rippled across his backside with each forward thrust she made like ocean waves of ecstacy. Odette couldn't help but admire his flexibility. He had his face completely buried in another moaning woman's cunt while craning his arms back to spread his ass. The screams of the woman whose pussy was being devoured were muffled by the balls she was being forced to suck. The other man was on his knees above her face, hands on his hips. Every time the woman would release his balls for air, he would thrust his hips forward, sharply, so they would clap her in the face. Odette let her hand drift down the smooth wood of the doorframe when the man turned his head slightly. Slightly was all she needed to go from Niagara Falls to a puff of dust.

Brom... and neither of those women were Katrina. The bastard left her at home to do chores and look after the baby while he got his dick wet. Why couldn't she enjoy this, too?

Odette's stomach churned. She closed her eyes and wished someone would castrate that fucking pig. She reached into the hidden pocket of her dress and pulled out the folded piece of paper, the words Joan of Arc were written in bold, dark strokes. Her heart began to pound as she walked deeper into the house, the moans and laughter fading to a low, pulsing thrum in her ears. She stopped in front of the door marked with that name and opened it.

Inside, the room was lit by dozens of candles, their light casting a warm, flickering glow over the dark wood and heavy tapestries. The air was even thicker here, the scent of sweat and perfume curling in her lungs, the shadows of lovers playing out across the walls in endless, shifting patterns.

Ellis stood at the center of it all, leaning against the carved bedpost with a lazy, hungry smile. He was already nude, cock hard. His piercing green eyes caught the candlelight. The planes of his lean body bathed in gold like a Greek god. The veins that danced down his forearms were visible as he watched her. His light brown hair was tousled, and he looked every inch the rake she'd first met at the masquerade ball held just the spring before, all effortless charm. He was a writer for the Hudson Valley Post and was there to report on the dancing and goings on at the ball.

Although, Odette didn't quite know how much information he got since he spent most of the time with her.
They had never bothered with love. Neither of them wanted it. What they wanted was this. All the heat. All the sweat. All the sex.
She let her lips curl into a slow smile, her hips swaying as she stepped inside, closing the door behind her. He pushed off the bedpost and met her halfway, his hands sliding around her waist, his breath warm against her ear.

"Joan of Arc tonight?" he murmured.

She tipped her head back, her smile deepening. "I'll be your saint if you'll be my sin."

His laughter was soft, his mouth finding hers in a kiss that tasted of whiskey and hunger. In the flickering candlelight, the world outside the room slipped away. She let herself melt against him, her heart beating wildly. She was the black swan tonight. That meant no mercy.
"Oui, Maitresse," She whispered before Ellis slipped her dress off with expert precision.

He spit in his hand and rubbed it in between her thighs, paying special attention to her already engorged clit. He pushed her onto the bed and threw her legs over his shoulders. Before she could even moan, he slid into her. "I've been waiting for your pussy all night," he said, thrusting forward. She felt her ass lift off the bed and her knees come closer to her ears.

'Tais-toi et baise-moi," she said, breath becoming more ragged.

Then she saw something in his eyes snap as his hand shot forward grasping her throat just enough to make her eyes widen.

"You just got wetter around my cock. Try telling me to shut up again and see what happens. I will leave you half wrecked, Odette."

Odette smirked.

She liked it when Ellis was this way.

Just when she thought his power thrusts in combination with a pinch of dominance were going to be the recipe for her orgasm, he pulled out. His cock was dripping wet and rock hard. He slammed her legs down on the bed and flipped her on her belly- effortlessly. Then he grabbed her hips, nails digging into her skin as he pulled her ass towards him and positioned the tip of his cock at the entrance of her tightest hole. Then he slowly pushed in, letting her stretch around him.

In all honesty, Odette had bigger dicks in France, but Ellis knew how to make her cum.

He started slowly, but each thrust had gusto behind it. It made her ass cheeks jiggle with reverberation and she could feel it in her clit. So she reached a hand between her thighs and began to massage it in slow circles. She felt her orgasm building and her walls began to pulsate. Ellis felt it, too, and sped up his rhythm.

Grunting, groaning, and finally a sharp gasp as he came. Odette cried out as she felt his hot liquid spilling into her asshole. She rode the waves of her orgasm until they both collapsed in a heaping pile of sweat on the bed.

Odette pushed the entangled feet of another couple off one of the white, goose feather pillows so she could lay her head.

Odette lay sprawled across Ellis's chest, skin slick with sweat, breath slowly evening out. The sheets were half off the bed, tangled around their legs, and his fingers traced lazy patterns down the curve of her spine.

"Goddamn," he muttered, voice still gravely. "You're dangerous."

She smiled against his skin. "Takes one to know one."
Ellis reached over the edge of the bed and dug through
the mess of his clothes on the floor. He came up with a
silver case, cool and elegant in his palm. He flipped it
open and plucked a cigarette from inside. The tobacco
was encased in thin, dark paper, rolled tight by hand.
Definitely smuggled. He struck a match off the bedpost,
flame flaring gold in the candlelight.

The scent of clove and tobacco filled the room- smoky,
rich, spiced like pumpkin pie. He took a long drag, then
held it out to her.

She took it, brushed her fingers against his, and pulled a
puff deep into her lungs. The smoke bit, but she exhaled
like a queen, her lips parting in a soft, satisfied sigh.

"Thanks," she said, standing up and reaching for her
dress. "But I've got to go."

Ellis sat up, frowning, the sheet sliding down his hips
exposing his cut lines. "You're fucking mad."

She raised a brow at him. "Excuse me?"

"You heard me," he said, cigarette between his lips
again. "It's almost midnight. The schoolhouse is over the
goddamn bridge and through the woods. You really
want to go wandering through the forest in that little
dress with your tits still red from where I bit you?"

Odette smirked. "Perle knows the way."

"You think that horse is going to save you from the
Horseman?"

She pulled her stays tight and turned to him with a sharp laugh. "Don't start with that bullshit."

"I'm serious."

"You're full of shit."

He got out of bed, completely naked, smoke curling around him like a demon in heat. "You don't believe in ghost stories?"

"No, Ellis. I don't believe in your spooky little legends. Just because this town loves to finger-fuck its own folklore doesn't mean I have to believe in it."

"You should."

She pulled on her boots. "And why is that?"

"Because he's real. The Headless Horseman isn't some nursery rhyme. He rides when the moon's high and the forest's asleep. Tonight's one of those nights."

Odette sighed. "Please, not this again."

"Ichabod Crane?" Ellis snapped. "Gone. Just gone. Vanished in the dark with nothing left but a floating hat and a smashed pumpkin. And he's not the only one. There've been others. Drunks, lovers, travelers. Hell, even that idiot senator. No one who enters the woods at midnight comes out whole."

She crossed her arms, skeptical. "You're just trying to scare me into staying."

"I'm trying to keep your gorgeous ass alive."

He walked toward her, still bare, eyes dark.

"He rides when the moon is high,
Keep to your path and don't meet his eye.
For he who strays beneath branches wide
May never again reach the other side.
Don't turn back for a second look.
Head for the bridge above the brook.
Cross the bridge if you want to return.
So he doesn't kill you with his jack 'o' lantern."

She rolled her eyes, laughing. "God, you're dramatic."

"I'm not fucking joking, Odette."

"I'll be fine," she said, grabbing her cloak. "Me and Perle are not scared of fairytales."

She stepped outside before he could say another word. Eyes lightening. Shame setting in.

The white swan was back in control.

The air was thick with heat and smoke and the wet perfume of sex. Naked bodies were still wrapped around each other on velvet cushions and half-collapsed chaises, moaning or passed out under the stars. Candles guttered in lanterns. Someone laughed as a woman rode a man's face in the grass.

Odette didn't look twice. She was already at the forest's edge where Perle had been tied.

The mare stamped her foot, uneasy, ears pricked toward the dark trees.

"Don't you start," Odette whispered.

Then she heard it. A laugh. Not soft. Not human. A sharp, cutting sound that echoed straight out of the woods.

Perle reared back, let out a shrill whinny, and broke free, hooves crashing against the earth as she ran straight into the forest.

"Perle!" Odette shouted, bolting after her, skirts clutched in one hand, cloak trailing behind her. "You stupid bitch, get back here!"

She hit the bridge at full speed. The wood creaked under her boots, the air colder now, like ice down her spine.

She was in the forest. At midnight.

The trees swallowed her whole. The candlelight and laughter behind her vanished like smoke. Shadows thickened. The air turned wet. She couldn't even hear her own footsteps.

Only the pounding of her heart.

Deeper in the woods...another laugh.

Closer.
Odette tried her hardest to rationalize it, but she couldn't think of a bird in the world that made that sound.

She walked as fast as she could toward the schoolhouse, her boots snapping against the narrow dirt path, cloak clutched around her shoulders. The forest swallowed the moonlight, branches overhead gnarled like the twisted fingers of the dead. Every shadow seemed to reach for her, and the trees groaned in the breeze like they were whispering secrets meant to stay buried.

"Fucking hell," she muttered, eyes darting ahead for any sign of Perle. "Perle, you whore-"

A branch lashed out, catching her skirts. She yanked but it held tight, thorns catching the delicate fabric. When she twisted to free herself, her boot slipped, and she went down hard. Knees to dirt, hands scraped raw.

The wind stopped. The forest was dead silent.

She looked up and her blood turned to ice.

There, no more than twenty yards ahead, stood a horse–black as the void behind closed eyes, muscles thick and gleaming like oil beneath the moonlight that should not have reached this deep into the trees. Its nostrils flared, expelling clouds of mist that curled, rising around it as though it had crawled up from hell itself.

Sitting astride it was the Horseman.
His coat was military-cut, pristine and perfectly tailored, dark velvet with silver buttons that shimmered in the thin light. It clung to his frame, elegant and fearsome, all the way up to the sharp slope of his shoulders- where a head should have been. Just

emptiness. Like the body had been carved clean by some vengeful god.

Odette couldn't breathe.

Her lungs hitched, catching on nothing. Her chest rose and fell in rapid gasps, and her fingers dug into the cold dirt. Her mouth opened but no sound came out. Her heart was trying to climb up her throat.

The Horseman didn't move. But his horse did.

It reared back onto its hind legs, hooves flailing in the air like blades. The scream it let out wasn't equine…it was something not of this world. It sounded like a man being gutted.

Then it charged.

"Shit! Shit! Fuck!" Odette scrambled to her feet, yanking her dress free with a loud tear. Lace ripped, and fabric tangled around her legs, but she ran. The forest blurred past her, trees like black bars, the pounding hooves behind her shaking the earth.

She could hear it breathing.

Could feel it. Hot, sulfuric, like death breathing down her neck.

The bridge, her mind screamed. Get to the fucking bridge.

Branches tore at her arms, her hair, her dress. One of her boots came loose and she nearly fell again, but she slipped it off and kept running, wild, blind, desperate.

She saw it...

The narrow silhouette of the bridge cut through the forest like salvation at a cathedral.

Her legs burned. Her chest was tight. But she pushed harder, feet slamming the planks just as a gust of wind blew the scent of scorched leather and smoke past her face.

She crossed.

The second her feet hit the other side, everything stopped.

Dead quiet.

She turned around, panting, eyes wide, body shaking with adrenaline and terror.

He stood on the other side.

Still.

His body faced hers, perfectly still atop the demonic beast beneath him. The horse pawed the ground once, steam still rising from its nostrils.

And though he had no head...nothing at all atop those broad, immaculate shoulders...Odette swore he was staring at her.

Something in the shape of him felt... sad. Trapped.
Bound to this side and unable to cross over.

She felt the weight of his longing in the way his torso
leaned toward her, his broad chest angled forward as if
pulled by something he could not resist. His horse stood
eerily calm beneath him, hooves quiet against the earth.
The glow of his pumpkin softened, no longer wild or
threatening, but warm, casting a gentle amber light
across her face.

She blinked, chest still heaving.

When she opened her eyes again, he was gone.
Just the empty forest and the soft creak of the bridge
behind her. The silence throbbed.

Odette let out a breath she hadn't realized she was
holding.

Then she turned and walked toward the schoolhouse,
half her dress torn to shreds, mud streaked across her
skin, and Ellis's words ringing in her ears.

You're mad.

Maybe he was right. Maybe she was.

"Do you believe in ghost stories now?"

"Oui, maîtresse."

Chapter 4

Son Fantôme

(Phantom Son)

Odette hadn't slept. Not really. She'd sat in the corner of the schoolhouse wrapped in a moth-eaten quilt with the lamps burning low, thinking of him. Of the Horseman. The steam rising from the horse's nostrils. The sound of hooves like war drums behind her. The way he just... stood there.

If he'd had a head, she thought, his eyes would've been on me.

They wouldn't have been cruel.

They would have been longing.

Which is exactly why, after scrubbing herself clean and shoving her blonde hair beneath a scarf, she rode the cowardly bitch, Perle, into town and stormed into the Hudson Valley Post, the stink of ink and pipe smoke wafting through the swinging doors.

Ellis sat behind a brown wooden desk, shirt open at the throat, vest barely buttoned, suspenders hanging at his hips like the sexy gentleman he was.

"Well," he said, not even looking up, "if it isn't the girl who doesn't believe in ghost stories."

"I changed my mind," she snapped, yanking the scarf off her head and tossing it onto the desk.

Ellis raised an eyebrow. "What happened? Did the phantom give you a little midnight kiss?"

"I saw him," she said, sitting on the desk right in front of him, legs crossed high enough to make a priest drop his pants and sin right there. "He saw me. I want to know who the hell he is and why he's still on this plane of existence."

Ellis leaned back, a slow grin tugging at the corners of his mouth. "You always get this worked up when you're scared or just when you're turned on?"

"Both," she said, cold as ass on ice. "But if you help me dig through the archives and figure out who he is, I'll let the Black Swan thank you properly."
He blinked. "You serious?"

"She does give better head."

Ellis laughed. "God, I love this fucking town."

They went to work.

He led her past the typesetters and into the archive room. The dusty shelves stacked with yellowed editions and brittle press sheets going back to before the revolution. It smelled like mold. Odette rolled up her sleeves.

It was nearly two days before Ellis sucked in a breath. "Here."

She knelt beside him, reading over his shoulder. The page was dated November 1776, printed in cramped type and fading ink. The headline read:

BLOOD ON WHITE PLAINS: THE CARNAGE OF THE HESSIAN LINE

The byline belonged to a man named Jonathan Briggs, a journalist from Albany who had traveled to the front lines to document the battle.

"Listen to this," Ellis said.

Among the Hessian forces, one name rose in whispers among soldiers on both sides- Steffan Weber. A soldier unmatched, a blade so fast and merciless he left no survivors to speak of him. His command was loyal, until betrayal struck not from the enemy, but from within. A cannonball obliterated his head mid-charge. His horse crushed beside him. No burial. No marker. Just smoke and silence. The forest swallowed him.

Odette stared at the name. Steffan Weber. It rang in her head like a bell tolling for the dead.

"He never made it back," she whispered. "No one brought him home. No one mourned him."

"No one even tried to find him," Ellis said. "They left him to rot in those woods."

She leaned back against the shelf. "White Plains is only a few miles from here. The forest he rides in connects straight to the old battlegrounds."

Ellis nodded slowly, his grin gone. "He's still looking."

"For his head," she said. "For revenge."

Odette could feel her pulse in her throat. It was real. All of it was real.

Then she remembered the way the Horseman had stood at the edge of the bridge. The sorrow. The stillness. That ache of being stuck.

"We have to help him cross over," she said.

Ellis looked at her sideways, that lazy, crooked grin pulling back into place.

"I may be able to help with that, too," he said, smugly. "But... what's in it for me?"

Odette turned slowly, her skirt brushing against his knee, her shadow swallowing his boots. She stared at him, face unreadable.

Her eyes darkened.

"I'll let you tie me to the bed and use the horse crop on my ass," she said simply, pulling the article from his hands and folding it with brutal precision.

Ellis's brows jumped. "Fuck."

She leaned down so her lips brushed the shell of his ear. "Yes, but I will not bend over for you until we find out what he wants."

Ellis swallowed thickly, eyes a little glazed, like a man half-drowned in lust. "Deal."

She turned on her heel, already moving toward the door when he called after her.

"There's someone you need to meet," he said. "I wrote about her a few months back. Bit of a local legend. Real gypsy shit."

She paused. "You mean Romani?"

"Yeah, yeah. Romani. Michelle. Her people don't stay in one place long, but she's got a caravan set up off Hollow Creek. Told me she was passing through, but that was three years ago." He smirked. "The town wouldn't let her go. Not after she helped Mrs. Telford find her dead husband's spirit hiding in her goddamn attic."

Odette raised a brow. "A seer?"

"A real one," Ellis said. "Says she sees the dead, talks to 'em, helps 'em cross. Or keeps them here if they're not ready."

Odette tucked the article beneath her arm. "She might know how to help Steffan."

Ellis stood, stretching, shirt riding up just enough to tease the lines along his hips. "Oh, she'll help. Especially if I ask."

"And what exactly did you do for her the last time?" Odette asked, lip curling.

He grinned. "Nothing that can't be repeated."

Odette rolled her eyes but didn't argue.

Michelle.

If anyone knew what that Horseman wanted…what tied him to this cursed stretch of land…it would be someone like her. A woman between astral planes.

In the back of her mind, she saw him again. Steffan. Silent on the other side of the bridge, that headless body somehow watching her, waiting.

If he'd had eyes, they would've been sad.

If he still had a voice, he might've begged her to free him.

Romani camp was tucked deep beyond Hollow Creek, half-hidden behind hanging moss and rustling oaks. Lanterns swayed from crooked poles. Crimson and violet scarves fluttered in the breeze. The scent of smoke, and bone dust hung in the air like a strong perfume.

Michelle's caravan was painted a deep blue and adorned with constellations. When she opened the door, it was like she had parted and walked through the night sky.

She was stunning.

Black curls spilled over her shoulders in a cascade of silk, eyes like molten gold, wrapped in layers of velvet and leather. Bangles clinked when she moved, and her smile was sharp enough to slice the seam of any man's ballsack.

"Ellis," she purred, leaning in close. "Back to sniff around my skirts?"

Ellis gave her a roguish grin. "Only when they smell like your cunt."

Michelle laughed low, almost like a growl, "You'll need to get on your knees if you want me to throw my ass around today!"

"Ahem," Odette cleared her throat.

Michelle's eyes flicked to Odette. "I see you've brought a friend."

"I saw him," Odette stated.

"Saw who?" Michelle's eyes narrowed.

'The Horseman," Odette said. Her voice didn't tremble. "I think he needs help."

A crow screeched in the distance. Michelle tilted her head just slightly, studying Odette like she was reading something scrawled in invisible ink across her skin.

"You saw him? Not just a blur in the trees or some shadow on a hill? You looked at him?"

Odette nodded. "He showed himself to me.He wasn't just mist. He had a body! He was on his horse!"

Michelle took a slow step forward, her bracelets clinking like tiny bells. She circled Odette once, fingers twitching like she could feel the energy pouring off her. When she stopped, her voice was quiet but heavy with meaning.

"You're split."

Odette blinked. "Excuse me?"

Michelle's mouth twitched into the barest smirk. "You carry two lives in one body. The innocent and the wild. The teacher and the temptress."

Ellis coughed behind them. "She's definitely got a temper."

Michelle didn't look at him. She was still locked in on Odette. "That's why he came to you. That's why he could. Spirits like that... they don't show themselves unless something pulls them through. He didn't just want to be seen. He wanted to be understood. And something in you...maybe both parts of you...called him."

Odette blinked. "You think I can help him?"

"I think you might be the only one who can," Michelle said. "You'll need both sides. One to see him clearly... and one to face what he's become."

Ellis whistled low. "Shit. That sounds dangerous."

Michelle shrugged. "Most real things are."

"So will you help us or not?" Odette asked.

Michelle didn't hesitate. "We'll need fire, salt, and blood."

They met that night at the edge of the forest, where the trees turned to claws and the wind blew colder than it had any right to in October.

Michelle knelt in a wide circle drawn in salt. Tall candles lit the perimeter, their flames dancing. She chanted under her breath in a language neither Ellis nor Odette could place.

Odette stood just outside the circle, the article about Steffan clutched in her hand. Her pulse pounded at her temple. Ellis stood beside her, hands in pockets, trying not to look nervous.

Michelle drew her bejeweled dagger across the pad of her thumb, letting the blood drip into the fire.

"I call you, rider of the Hollow," she murmured. "I call you, soldier lost to betrayal. I call you, Steffan Weber…"

The flames danced. Smoke coiled.

Nothing.

The wind died.

The woods grew still.

Dead silence.

Michelle's brow furrowed. "He doesn't want to come."

"Why not?" Odette demanded, stepping closer.

"He's resisting."

Odette looked toward the trees.

"Then I'll go to him. He showed himself to me once."

Michelle looked up sharply. "Don't you dare."

Ellis reached to grab her arm. "Odette. This is fucking suicide."

But she was already stepping across the salt line, boots crunching against brittle leaves. She walked straight to the bridge, chin high, breath shallow.

She crossed it.

Everything in the forest shifted. An invisible weight dropping around her shoulders, a breathless, heavy stillness.

Odette looked out into the dark, voice steady but soft.

"Steffan."

The mist gathered like smoke off a dying battlefield. A swirl of it rose from the ground, thick and curling. Forming into a man's shape.

He appeared like a nightmare out of fog. He was broad, powerful, cloaked in midnight with black riding gear. The coat clung to him, pristine. Elegant. His shoulders broad.

Odette's mouth opened to scream, but nothing came out.

His head began to materialize..First shadow. Then bone. Then skin. High cheekbones. A strong jaw. Mouth drawn in sorrow. And his eyes...

God, his eyes.

The color of lightning. Like shattered silver.

So handsome, it knocked the breath from her lungs.

Odette took one step back, then another, lips parted in awe and fear.

Then everything went white.

She dropped to the grass with a thud. From the other side of the bridge, Ellis shouted her name in panic.

"Odette!"

She crumpled in the dirt, her limbs limp, blonde curls spilling around her face. The mist swallowed her whole. "Fuck this," Ellis growled and started forward.

Michelle yanked him back, her fingers like iron around his arm. "No. Don't. Not past the bridge. Not unless you've got a death wish."

He spun on her. "He's got her!"

"He won't hurt her," she said, staring into the smoke like she knew something he didn't. "Not her."

Ellis cursed under his breath. "What the fuck do you mean 'not her'?"

But she didn't answer.

They both watched, helpless, as the Horseman appeared fully now- towering, terrifying, his eyes shining through the fog like polished metal. He bent low, scooped Odette up like she weighed nothing, and swung her body over his horse.

The beast snorted, steam curling from its nostrils. Its hooves pawed the earth. Muscles like shadows rippled beneath jet-black skin. It was wrong...something carved from a nightmare.

Ellis's breath hitched. "He's not supposed to be that solid."

Michelle was pale, chest heaving. "She said his name. It pulled him closer to this Earth. Closer to her."

The Horseman turned slowly, facing them across the bridge. His body was still. His face...beautiful in the most fucked up way. Tragic. Cold. Like a man who'd forgotten how to be anything but haunted.

He looked straight at them.

If he had a voice, Ellis was sure he'd say, "She's mine, fool."

Then the horse turned.

With a violent jerk of its head, it disappeared into the woods, mist trailing behind it like a veil.

Michelle's grip loosened, her voice barely a whisper. "Shit. We've got a problem."

Chapter 5

À Mi-chemin Libre

(Halfway Free)

The world was black and moving fast.

Odette's eyes snapped open and the first thing she saw was the blank space where a head should be. Just a torso in a dark, pristine Hessian coat. Brass buttons polished, not a single rip in the stitching. That coat told the truth. This was no wandering spirit. He was a soldier still, a ghost of war living in the New England mist.

Her eyes widened and she shrieked.

Her body jerked in panic. She slipped from the saddle and tumbled off the side like a ragdoll, hitting the ground hard. Her shoulder took most of it, then her hip, then her back. Mud clung to her skin. Her breath came in panicked gasps as she lay there, dress torn, chest heaving, staring up in horror.

The black horse skidded to a halt just ahead, steam rising off its back. Its hooves stomped the earth, eyes glowing, a monstrous silhouette against the trees. It snorted once and turned back.

Then he dismounted the horse.

The Headless Horseman.

Steffan.

He moved slow, smooth, calm as hell. He picked up the pumpkin, his goddamn jack-o'-lantern, and placed it on the ground again like it was the most precious thing he ever touched.

Then he walked toward her.

She couldn't fucking move. Not her legs, not her arms, not her mouth. She was frozen. Her heart was doing somersaults and her mind was screaming at her to run.

Odette tried to get up, legs shaky, breath still ragged, dress torn to shit. She pushed off the ground with all the dignity she had left...only for her heel to catch on the hem of her skirt. Her foot slid. Her arms flailed.

She went down again with a graceless thump, landing face-first in the dirt and ass-up like some tragic heroine who'd had one too many drinks at the town masquerade.

"Fucking hell," she groaned into the ground, gravel in her mouth and humiliation in her bones. Even the wind seemed to laugh at her, rustling the leaves just loud enough to be a little bitch about it.

She rolled over and sat up only to come face to figurative face with a kneeling torso.

She couldn't breathe...

Then she blinked and when she opened her eyes again, she was looking at the most striking face.

He had an immaculate, strong jawline, cheekbones that could cut glass, dark hair tied back but a few strands falling loose around his face.

He stayed kneeling in front of her, tilting his ghostly head just enough to make it feel like he was drinking her in, like he had all the time in the fucking world to memorize her.

His eyes dragged over her body like a damn caress lingering on the dip of her waist then traveling to the dirt-smeared curve of her thigh and the rise and fall of her chest as she tried to catch her breath.

He didn't touch her, but the way he looked at her made her feel stripped bare like every inch of her was his to study. It was filthy. The kind of stare that turned her pussy into a waterfall.

When his gaze finally landed on her face it held there hungry as hell like he was trying to figure out what kind of woman would call out to the dead and make him want to come crawling back to life.

It was like lightning struck every inch of her body when he looked at her with those pale eyes. Odette can barely peg them on the color spectrum.

"Who are you," he said.

His voice was like smoke…thick, deep, and sexy. It had a warmth to it, like the flicker of a jack-o'-lantern flame glowing behind a crooked smile. Each word felt like embers. Soft at first, then burning slow, leaving the scent of scorched autumn aromas.

She swallowed. He could fucking talk…

Her voice was barely working, but she managed to whisper her name. "Odette."

Something passed through his expression when he heard her name. Like it hurt.

Her breathing was ragged. A legend that wasn't supposed to exist was right in front of her.

She was terrified. Shaking.

His eyes softened.

"Don't be afraid, Odette," he said.

The way he said her name sent shivers down her spine.

"Why do you keep coming here, Odette? Calling out a
ghost's name like you're begging him to answer."

"I-I.." she stuttered.

"People lose their heads in these woods, you know?" he
said as he reached out a gloved hand and lifted her chin.
'Yet here you are offering yours on a platter."

She just stared at him and gulped. It was embarrassing
really. She usually never had a problem speaking, but
damn, she did not expect him to be this fucking sexy.

"I told you not to be afraid, Odette." His voice blew a
hole in her thoughts.

"I know who you are," she said. "You're Steffan Weber
and you were betrayed at White Plains."

His eyes flared.

"I read about you," she whispered. "I've seen you."
He studied her for a moment, then sat back on his heels.
"You didn't scream when you first saw me. Not really.
You looked at me like you knew me."

She pushed herself up with a grunt. Her shoulder ached
like hell.

"Maybe I did."

He looked her over. Not in a creepy way, not just lust. Like he was reading her. Trying to see something beneath her porcelain skin.

"You called me by name. How long have you been able to speak to the dead?"

" I thought I could help you," she said.

His voice dropped low. "That doesn't answer my question."

Silence stretched.

Then he reached for her. She let him. Soft fingers grazing her chin, brushing dirt from her cheek. His touch wasn't cold. It was warm. Warm like he'd stolen it from the fires burning in hell.

"You saw me," he said. "But that's not the reason I took you."

She held still, caught under his gaze.
"There's something about you, Odette," he murmured. "Something that called me closer. Something I've been waiting to feel for a long fucking time."

Her breath shook. "You're not just looking for your head?"

"No." His face twisted. "That's the story they tell to scare the piss out of children so they'll go to sleep. I'm looking for something worse."

"Then what are you looking for?"

He exhaled, and his voice took on a bitter sound. "Justice."

He stood slowly, his hand slipping down her arm as he helped her to her feet again. His eyes burned.

"They betrayed me. My own. At White Plains. They made a deal behind closed doors. Sold me out. I was killed by my own men. Adderley made sure of that."

"I'm sorry," she said, voice breaking. "I know what betrayal feels like."

His head tilted, that flicker of softness returning. "I believe you, Odette."

She didn't pull away when his hand touched her waist. Didn't stop him when his other hand slid behind her neck.

"So you're not afraid of me?" He whispered.

"Should I be,?" She replied. He left her breathless.

He leaned in until his lips brushed her temple. "Maybe."

She swallowed hard, heart pounding.

"But if you really want to help me, Odette," he said, voice like smoke, "then stay with me a little longer. Let me show you where it started."

"Where?"

He looked back toward the trees. The fog was starting to move again.

"The battlefield," he said. "You want to break my curse and set me free? You've got to see where it was born."

She hesitated. Then nodded.

He mounted the horse again and offered her his hand. She took it without hesitation.

But this time, she held on tighter.

The ride through the fog was fucking intoxicating. The wind was cold against her skin. The scent of raw earth and wet leaves filled her lungs. Odette clung to Steffan, arms locked tight around his waist as the black horse devoured the mist like some demon creature out of a nightmare. Every muscle of his back flexed beneath her fingertips. She could feel him. Alive. Dangerous. Barely contained.

"What's his name?" she asked, her voice soft, brushing her cheek against the leather of his coat.

"Nacht," Steffan murmured. "It means night."

She smiled darkly. "Of course it does."

Her breath ghosted across his shoulder. "I've always felt like there's something inside me too. A darker side. Something that doesn't belong in the daylight. I call her the Black Swan."

He pulled back slightly. Slowed the horse. Looked at her like he could see through her skin.

"The Black Swan," he repeated, tasting the words like fine wine. "Then let me meet her one day. I want to know everything about the woman who isn't afraid of me. There's beauty in darkness. You just have to feel around for it. Sometimes the darkest thing we fear about ourselves is the thing that makes us unforgettable."

Her heart kicked hard and fell into her ass because that was one of the most beautiful fucking things Odette- had ever heard.

They broke through the last of the trees. The fog rolled thin and broken as the land opened into a dead stretch of earth. Silent. Still. Heavy and haunted.

"White Plains," Steffan said as he slid off the horse. His boots sank into the frost-bitten grass. "This is where I died. Where everything twisted into what I am."

She followed. The air tasted wrong. It was like there was no life. No birds chirping. No bugs on the ground. Nothing.

"I trusted him," Steffan said. His voice wasn't calm. It wasn't anything close to calm. "Brigadier General Adderley. I bled for him. I fought beside him. I would have died for him."

Her stomach twisted. "What happened?"

He laughed. Bitter. Cold. "He fed me straight into hell. Told me to ride ahead. He knew what was waiting for me in the ravine. I was a pawn in whatever fucking deal he made for power. For glory."

Her breath caught.

"I've heard the stories over the years. I know he's not at rest. I can feel it," said Steffan. "If that bastard's ghost is still out here rotting in this dirt, I'll find him. I'll drag his spirit screaming into the next life. Only then can I leave. Only then can the ghosts of Sleepy Hollow be nothing more than a fucking bedtime story."

The look in his eyes was wild. Starving. Shattered. It should have terrified her.

She reached for him instead. "Then we'll find him. I swear it."

The air between them cracked open. She didn't see him move. One second she was breathing and the next his mouth was on hers. Their teeth clashed. Their tongues explored. Their breath tangled. Her warm lips were the perfect natural enemy to his cold mouth. It wasn't gentle. It was madness and savagery at the same time.

She didn't want gentle. She wanted this.

His hands were everywhere. Her waist. Her thighs. Her hair. He dragged her down to the frost bitten ground and pressed into her until she felt him in every fucking cell of her body. She arched against him. Moaned into his mouth. When his fingers slid under her skirts she gasped. Heat shot through her as he effortlessly found her already soaked pussy.

"Fuck, Odette," he whispered, teeth grazing her skin.

"You're drenched for me... would you like the headless horseman to collect what's his?"

With that, he began lightly stroking her already swollen clit with his index finger.

She gasped.

His touch was so cold now. It was like her whole body was just shoved inside a ghost's ass, but honestly, she wasn't mad about it. He felt that good.

Her hips rolled against his hand as he teased her. Cruel. Perfect. She could barely think. Could barely breathe. She was clutching his coat like it would keep her from flying into the fucking afterlife herself.

Then he shoved two fingers inside her and her body clenched down so hard it made her knees buckle. He started to pump them slow, like he wanted to savor every twitch of her cunt, curling them just enough to grind against that spot that made her head tip back, her mouth dropped open to emit a scream with no sound. His thumb pressed to her clit, rough and calloused, working messy circles that made her shake against him. His hands felt like they belonged to the dead, but fuck if they didn't know exactly how to wreck her.

Somewhere in the back of her mind she knew this wasn't real. Couldn't be real. He wasn't alive, he wasn't flesh, he wasn't supposed to know how to touch her like this. But he did. He knew too well. He knew how to tear her apart with nothing but his hand, knew how to make her gush so hard her thighs were sticky and her skirts stuck to her skin. She could hear it, the wet slap of his fingers working in and out of her, obscene and loud and it echoed between the trees like the forest itself was watching.

And still he didn't stop. She was soaked. The ground was soaked. She didn't even know if she was standing or if he was the only thing holding her up anymore.

His mouth pressed to her ear, his voice cold and sweet and filthy all at once.

"You poor thing. Drenched for a ghost. Do you even care if I haunt you forever? Or are you just going to let me fuck the life out of you?"

She didn't answer. She couldn't. She was already gone.

"Let go," he whispered. His breath was ragged. "I want to hear you. I want your whole body to sing for me."

Her body lit up. She came hard. A broken cry tore from her lips as he worked her through it. His mouth on her neck. His voice in her ear.

"Good girl...good girl...good fucking girl. Ride my fingers."

She was drowning in it. Every nerve in her body was burning at the end...

When her breath finally slowed he was still there. Still holding her. Still touching her like she mattered. He still had a head.

He kissed her forehead. His cold lips felt so good on her hot skin.

"Are you cold?" he asked.

"A little," she murmured, dazed.

He pulled her closer. His coat wrapped around both of them. "I don't mind the cold."

She pressed her palm to his chest. No heartbeat.

"We'll find him," she whispered. "I'll help you finish this. I swear it."

He kissed her temple. "Then I'm already halfway free."

The land held its breath. The only sound that broke the silence was the echo of Nacht's ghostly gallop back toward Sleepy Hollow.

Chapter 6

La Faim et le Miroir

(Hunger and the Mirror)

Steffan

The forest was speechless. So was he.

Steffan crouched low beside a fallen log, his hands pressed into the cold earth, fingers digging into the rotted leaves like he needed to feel something pull back. Nothing did. Not tonight.

Nacht stood just behind him, ears twitching, his dark eyes reflecting the moonlight. The only one still willing to follow him into hell. Forever loyal.

His lips parted. His breath came slow. He couldn't form complete thoughts. He couldn't think.

All he knew was Odette.

The way she had looked at him.... like she'd been waiting for the monster in the woods to finally come for her.

He'd touched her like a savage. Finger fucked her like he was trying to crawl back into the living through her pussy. He was immediatly intoxicated by her voice and the way she begged for more...

He had sunk his fingers in and she let him.

Why?

Why the fuck did she let him?

Steffan rose abruptly and paced in a circle, dragging a hand through his long, black hair until he was clawing at his scalp. His throat burned. His chest ached. He couldn't breathe right, like he was choking on the memory of her moans. On the feel of her thighs clenching around his waist. On the way she had looked up at him, eyes glazed and unafraid, lips parted, ruined.

"I was supposed to haunt her," he growled into the dark. "Not crave her."

He was supposed to be done. A thing. A tale. A corpse that never found peace. Now it felt like blood burned in his veins like he was alive again, like she'd forced some sick imitation of life into him with every gasp, every slick squeeze of her cunt, every breathless whisper of his name.

He hated his need to have her...yet wanted it like a crow collecting shiny objects. He didn't know what he was going to do with her, but he had to have her.

Nacht huffed behind him.

Steffan turned to the horse, his voice a bitter rasp. "You saw her. You felt it too, didn't you? The way the Hollow pulled us toward her. Like it wants her."

He stared out into the trees, the moonlight broken across the forest like shattered glass. He wanted to tear the woods apart until something answered him. Until the Hollow coughed up its secrets and told him.

Why her?

Why now?

Odette

The candle was dying and honestly, so was she.

Odette sat in front of the mirror in her schoolhouse bedroom, knees pulled to her chest, hands twitching against the wood of her chair. She hadn't changed her clothes. Her thighs were still sticky. The remnants of Steffan's touch left a crude, humiliating throb between her legs.

She should have cried.

Instead she laughed once then slapped a hand over her mouth. Her reflection twitched in the candlelight. She stared into her own eyes. Maybe her own eyes.

"What the fuck is wrong with you, you casket cock warmer?" she whispered.

She had let a ghost shove his fingers inside her like she was nothing more than a cherry pie. And she liked it.

She had thanked him for it with her voice, her body, the mess she'd made at his feet.

"You're sick," she whispered to her reflection.

Her reflection moved.

Not the room. Not the light. The mirror.

Behind her...or inside her ...stood the Black Swan.

The Swan's head tilted. Its face was hers but wrong, like something rotten wearing her skin.

"There she is," the Black Swan purred. "The Hollow's little corpse-bride cumrag."

Odette didn't move.

"You thought you were special? Thought some monster finger-fucked you like that because he loved you? No, Odette. He did it because you're available. Because you're an unlocked door with a sign that says come inside if you know her name. And guess what? They all do."

"I'm not listening to you," said Odette as she covered her ears.

"Aren't you?" the Swan laughed. It was like teeth splitting through flesh. "You let me waltz in, bare-footed, blood-drunk, and I made a home in your skull. You didn't fight. You moaned. You like me writhing inside your mind, don't you? Because it means you don't have to carry the blame. Not for your thoughts. Not for your cravings. Not for the festering, dripping filth that keeps you up at night."

"Shut up."

"Or what? You'll cry? You'll scream? Tell me how you're going to find Adderley and save Steffan when you can't even save yourself. Face it. You're a cracked vessel. I'm the only thing keeping you full. You're mine. You were always mine."

Odette shot up so fast the chair slammed behind her. The sound was like a gunshot in an empty room. Her eyes stretched wide, her breathing so erratic it sounded like sobbing without the tears. Her hands shook, fists clenched so tight her nails dug into her palms.

"You don't own me," she hissed. "You never fucking did."

The Swan's chin lifted slowly, her gaze slicing into Odette like a butcher's hook sliding under skin to drag it back and expose every tendon and ligament. She did not blink. She did not need to. She only watched, smiling with her eyes, mouth tight like a line waiting to rupture.

"Then why am I the only one smiling in that mirror?" she whispered.

The Swan's face split. A slow stretch. Her lips peeled back, her cheeks dragging thin, the skin trembling like it might rip apart from the pressure. It was the sound of flesh separating from bone like wet rope. Her mouth opened too wide, beyond what a face was meant to hold. The corners of her mouth stretched toward her ears and further still, pulling until Odette thought she could hear the tendons strain and snap. There were too many teeth inside. Not straight or clean. They jutted out sharp, ragged as broken bones stuffed into meat.

Her eyes never smiled. They stared, black and bottomless, twin voids that glittered like oil on water, slick and dangerous. There was something moving behind them. Something that wanted out.

When she spoke, it was not a voice. It was the sound of something half-submerged in water, gurgling, choking, but never dying.

"There you are." she crooned. "I was starting to wonder what your fear would taste like fresh."
The Swan tilted her head slowly. That grin stretched wider, the skin of her face pulling tighter, like her skull might crack open just to let more of her out.

Odette screamed. She could not help it. The sound clawed up her throat and ripped free before she could bury it. She grabbed the candle and hurled it across the room. It smashed against the wall with a crack, wax splattering, glass exploding, flame sputtering out in a sharp hiss. The room went dark.

Except for the mirror.

Pale and silver. Cold as a corpse's breath. The light was wrong. Too soft and too sharp at once, like the shine on a freshly sharpened blade. The reflection was not hers anymore. It was hers. The Black Swan.

She had not moved. She stood inside the glass, waiting, patient, grinning like something that had already eaten but was still hungry.

Odette's body trembled. Her hands shook violently, her fingers curling in so tight her nails cut into her palms. Her chest burned, her breathing shallow and fast. Her legs felt loose, her knees ready to buckle. She wanted to run. But the mirror would follow. She knew it would. It would follow her in her dreams. Behind her eyes. Every time she blinked.

"I'm going to save Steffan," she hissed. "I'm going to find Adderley. I'll gut you out of me if I have to use my bare fucking hands!"

The Swan chuckled. It sounded like rotting flesh sliding over bones.

"You'll try," she whispered. "But you'll fail. You'll wear yourself thin, Odette. You'll break open. You'll crack like wet wood and bleed yourself dry. And when you do, when you're empty and starving, I'll still be here."

Her voice dripped with bile. Sick.

"I'll wear you down inch by inch. Thought by thought. Breath by breath. I'll peel you back until there's nothing left but me. Until your bones are my bones. Your skin is my skin. Your voice, my voice. And when you look in the mirror, there won't be a 'you' anymore. There'll only be me smiling back."

She leaned closer, her black eyes shining, her smile splitting wider.

"Isn't that what you want, little girl? To stop fighting? To lay down and let me take over completely? It's easier. It's a light in the dark."

Odette shook her head hard enough that her hair whipped her face.

"Shut up," she spat. "Shut the fuck up."

But the Swan only smiled. She pressed her hand to the glass and the surface rippled, dark veins spiderwebbing from her palm like the mirror was cracking beneath her touch.

"You'll beg for it," the Swan crooned. "You'll crawl to the glass and press your forehead to it. You'll whisper for me to come out. Or for me to let you in. Either way I win. You're already mine because you're weak. You're a vessel and nothing more. You don't even know who you are without me."

"I'm the girl who's going to burn you," Odette snapped back. Her voice was trembling, but she made it loud. Solid. Sharp like a knife she would shove between the Black Swan's ribs if she could.

The Swan laughed. A wet shriek. A sound that made Odette's stomach flip and twist like she might vomit.

"Burn me then," The Black Swan whispered. "Burn us both."

Odette stumbled back. She had to get out. She had to leave this room. She turned from the mirror, her face burning, her mouth tasting like metal and sour spit. Her legs threatened to give out but she forced herself forward.

She grabbed her boots with shaking hands. Shoved them on. Yanked her coat from the hook like it might tear apart in her grip.

She could not fight this alone. She could not keep pretending she was strong enough. She needed Ellis. Paranoid, brilliant Ellis who always knew something was wrong. She needed Michelle, with her books and her talismans and her knowing eyes.
She would win. She would drag the Swan out by the hair and cut its throat if that was what it took.

She flung open the door, ready to step out, ready to escape the dark and the grin and the teeth.

Then she heard the Black Swan's voice calling after her in the most taunting way possible.

"Run little girl. Run as far and as fast as you want. You'll still have to come home to the mirror."

Odette slammed the door behind her, her breath ragged, her hands damp with sweat. She did not look back. She could not.

She knew if she looked back the mirror would still be there and if she looked back long enough her reflection would smile first.

She was going to win this battle. Find Adderley. Save Steffan.

Fuck the Black Swan.

Chapter 7

La Rose en Verre

(The Glass Rose)

Odette woke up tangled in sweat-soaked sheets. She shoved her way out of bed, shaking. Not scared. Not exactly. Just... on edge. Like something inside her was close to snapping its leash.

She sat on the edge of the bed and stared at the wooden floor, blonde hair wild around her face, heart hammering against her ribs. The Black Swan was getting stronger. It's like she felt a hunger to take over Odette's body. She wasn't just some voice in the back of her head anymore. It was something breathing down her neck.

Odette ran her fingers through her hair and stood up fast. She had to do something. She needed help. She couldn't do this alone. How was she supposed to help Steffan break his curse when she was dealing with her own?

She needed Ellis.

She made her way to the Hudson Valley Post where she knew she would find him. She stepped inside and the bell over the door gave a pathetic little chime that made her instantly want to punch something.

Ellis was behind his desk, sleeves rolled up, shirt wrinkled like he'd slept in it. When he looked up at her, his jaw locked tight and he didn't say a damn word. Just went back to writing as dramatically as he possibly could.

"Ellis," she said carefully.

He didn't look at her. "What do you want?"

That tone made her stomach flip. Not with nerves. With rage. "I need your help."

He stood up so fast his chair creaked against the floor. "You need help? After what you've been fucking around with?"

She frowned. "What's your problem?"

"You are," he snapped. "You're my damn problem. You and that...thing. You went with him. It was your choice. You did this willingly."

Odette took a step forward, voice cold. "Steffan is not a thing. He's a man who was betrayed, cursed, and left to rot in a story that never fucking ends."

Ellis scoffed. "So he's a ghost with nice cheekbones and a vendetta. Suddenly you're all about it."

She bit back a growl. "I'm serious, Ellis. I need help finding Brigadier General Adderley's ghost. If we can find him, Steffan can finally get justice. He can move on."

"And what?" Ellis said, rounding the desk. "You get a haunted happily ever after?"

"I get answers," she snapped. " and I help someone who deserves peace."

"You're helping a fucking ghost who has killed, Odette. He's terrorized Sleepy Hollow for years!"

"Well you're being a fucking coward."

He got in her face, eyes blazing. "Don't you dare."

"Don't I dare?" She shoved him back a step. "You don't get to tell me what I can and can't do."

"I'm trying to keep you from getting dragged into hell."

"Well, too fucking late for that," she spat.

His jaw clenched. "Then maybe you need a fucking exorcism."

She laughed, bitter and wild. "If you won't help me, I'll ask Michelle."

"Good luck with that," he snapped. "You think the gypsy's gonna get involved in your little ghost romance? She'll probably tell you the same thing I just did. We were both terrified for you the other night!"

Odette turned away from him, furious. "At least she won't lie to my face and pretend it's about helping me when it's really just about your fucking pride."

"Fine," he shouted after her. "Go see Michelle. Let her pull you into one of her crystal ball circles. Let her tell you what a brave little medium you are."

She didn't turn back. Didn't even give him the satisfaction of slamming the door. She just left.

The walk to Michelle's place felt like miles. Her boots kicked up gravel. Her heart pounded so hard her ribs ached. The Black Swan didn't say a word. She didn't have to. Her presence pulsed through Odette's veins, simmering just under the surface of her skin.

Michelle opened the door before she knocked. The little house smelled like sage, rosewater, and rum. The gypsy woman was barefoot, her eyes dark and knowing, her pendant already glowing faintly against her chest.

"You look like you're about to scream or set something on fire," Michelle said with a small smile. "Come in. Let's fix it."

Odette followed her through the velvet curtains into a room lined with books, hanging herbs, and glowing candles. Michelle gestured for her to sit at the round table in the center. Everything in the room felt like it had a spirit.

"I need to find a ghost," Odette said without hesitation. "Adderley. He's the reason Steffan's stuck. I want to find him. I want to help Steffan destroy him."

Michelle nodded, calm and without judgment. "Then we'll call to him. But I need to hold your hand. The veil between worlds is thin. If you slip, even a little, something from the other side will pull you through."

They sat around a small circular table- fingers laced. The pendant glowed brighter between them.

"There's something else," Michelle said gently. "I can feel a shadow within you."

Odette didn't look away. "The Black Swan."

Michelle's eyes flickered. "Ah. Yes. Her."

"Can you see her?"

"I can feel her. She's not a ghost."

Odette's shoulders stiffened. "Then what the fuck is she?"

Michelle leaned in. "She's you."

"No," Odette said. "She's darker. Meaner. Sluttier for sure! She doesn't care who she hurts."

"She is still you," Michelle said. "You are a glass rose. And she is a petal. If you break, she breaks off. If you lose her, you lose part of yourself."

Odette's throat tightened. "Can't you get rid of her?"

"No. And you don't want to. She is not evil. She is not cursed. She is your edge. Your fury. Your fire. Learn to use her or she will use you."

Odette's eyes burned. "She feels like a fucking evil ghost."

"She's not," Michelle said firmly. "She's your power. She's your war cry when the world tries to silence you. Don't let her become a weapon against you. She is a split personality."

Odette swallowed hard. "You really think I can control her?"
Michelle smiled softly. "I think you can give that slut a hard spanking and she'll be calling you mistress in no time."

"You know, that's what I call her."

A beat of silence.

Michelle squeezed her hand. "Ready?"

Odette nodded.

Michelle pulled out a small silver bowl, filled it with water, and lit a black candle beside it. The flame twisted unnaturally.

Michelle's voice dropped into a rhythmic chant:

"By blood, by bone, by wind and flame
We call the spirit who bears the name
Adderley, crass and cruel
Come forth now and face your rule…"

The air in the room was suffocating. The pendant flashed. A gust of wind howled through the house, though no window was open.

Odette's grip tightened. Her skin felt stretched too thin. Her heartbeat pounded in her ears.

"Show yourself," Michelle whispered. "Come forward. Answer for what you did…"
The candle flared.

Then..nothing.

The flame stilled. The water cleared. The air lightened.

Michelle exhaled and opened her eyes. "He's not coming."

Odette stared at her. "Why not?"

"I don't know. He heard us. I know he did."

"He's being a little bitch. Just like he was in life!"

Footsteps thundered across the floorboards above. A door slammed.

Then a voice.

"You need to stop this right now."

Ellis stormed down the stairs like a fucking hurricane. His face was tight with fury. His eyes locked on Odette like she'd committed murder.

"Get out," Michelle snapped, rising to her feet. "You weren't invited."

"You don't know what you're messing with," Ellis growled.

Michelle stood. "Don't you ever fucking interrupt a spirit calling again. You could have ruined everything!"

"You think this is a game?" Ellis shouted. "You think this is some fun séance party? You're poking at shit that wants to hurt Odette. He's probably put some curse on her to make her do this!"

"Steffan wouldn't so that to me." Odette said through gritted teeth.

"And you believe that? He is a fucking murderer. Why are you instantly trusting him?" Ellis questioned. His voice laced with jealousy and panic.

"You don't get to tell me what to believe," she shouted back. "You don't get to control this."

"You want to dance with ghosts? Fine. But don't come crying when one of them drags your ass to hell."

She didn't answer him. She shoved past him so hard he stumbled.

∞ ∞ ∞

She stormed all the way back to the schoolhouse with rage in her teeth and lightning in her fucking bones. She needed something cold. Something strong. Something French.

She threw open the cabinets until she found the good absinthe. Poured it into a cracked glass, no sugar cube.

"Fuck it," she muttered and slammed it back. The burn hit her throat like the Headless Horseman himself had reached into her chest and yanked her soul through her esophagus just for fun.

She made another.

Michelle was right. The Black Swan wasn't a demon. She wasn't a ghost.

She was her. Just another part of her. A part of her that she would need to accept and control and if Ellis

85

thought he could scare her off, he had another thing coming.

She drained the second glass and laughed. Not pretty. Not gentle. It was a double- chinned, snort- filled kind of laugh.

No one was gonna stop her now.

Not even the fucking dead.

Chapter 8

Mets-toi à Genoux

(Get on Your Knees)

The sun rose lazy and golden over Sleepy Hollow, bleeding warmth across the frosty rooftop of the schoolhouse. Inside, Odette tried desperately to give a fuck about fractions.

"If Abigail has nine apples and she gives six to Thomas, what percentage does she have left?"

Blank stares. One child picked her nose. Another was slowly, methodically chewing on a quill.

Odette blinked. Her gaze drifted to the window.
She yearned for him like he had just popped her cherry.
That was the problem...and not just because that ship
had long passed.

Every time she tried to explain numerators and
denominators, her brain rerouted to Steffan pinning her
wrists above her head, whispering filthy words against
her throat. Her knuckles turned white around the chalk.

"Three, Jonathan. The answer is three. Now, please stop
trying to set your desk on fire."

The bell rang. Sweet, merciful hell. The children
stampeded out like the caged crotch goblins they were.

She slumped at her desk and whispered, "Useless to
him," then immediately smacked the heel of her hand
against her forehead.

She wouldn't be.

Twilight draped Sleepy Hollow in velvety pinks and
bruised purples. Odette stood before her mirror in the
schoolhouse's tiny quarters, tugging the last ribbon of
her pink dress into a tight bow. The lace trim skimmed
her legs and tits nicely. Her eyes were dark, wide, feral.
Pearl, the cowardly bitch of a horse, huffed dramatically
as she mounted.

"You better not buck me off tonight," Odette muttered,
patting her neck. "I've got plans that don't include
getting my cunt broken. Might need that to be in tip-top
shape for later."

The bridge creaked under Perle's hooves. Odette stared straight ahead, heart hammering with the kind of anticipation that made her bones itch. The forest beyond loomed like It was ready to swallow her and keep her there forever.

Steffan and Nacht were waiting.

He was leaning against a tree, his cloak draped dramatically over one shoulder like some gothic prince of sexy nightmares. Nacht stood quietly beside him, steam curling from his nostrils like he was chewing through rage just to be still.

"You're late," Steffan said.

"You're lucky I came at all," she snapped, dismounting. Perle immediately backed up five paces, muttering horse obscenities under her breath.

Steffan smiled. It wasn't kind. It was lust and threat all wrapped in a very sexy and ghostly body. "Update. Now."

She exhaled, already bristling. "Adderley's ghost knows what's going on. That's all I have. I went to see a gyspsy, Michelle."

That got his attention. "A gypsy?"
"She prefers 'seer,' but yes. She's on our side. She can speak to the spirit world."

He nodded. That wasn't nothing. But his eyes narrowed.

"What aren't you telling me?"

Odette looked away.

"Odette."

She flinched. He crossed to her in two long strides, cupping her face in his gloved hand.

"Don't shut me out. I gave you the worst of me at White Plains. Let me see yours."

She cracked. She told him about the Black Swan. About the way Michelle said it was her and always had been. A creature. A shadow. A wound. A shield. She told him that she had fought it for years, but it never went away.

"And now?"

"Now... I think I have to let her out. Or it'll eat me alive."

Steffan's gaze burned into hers.

"Let her out. Show me. Let her rip me apart. I want to be devoured by her. You think your Black Swan scares me? I lost my head again long before I ever climbed onto that damned horse. I gave it to you, Odette. I just didn't know it."

He pulled her against him, his mouth crashing onto hers. It wasn't a kiss, it was a battle of tongues. She whimpered into it, clawed his coat, and pushed him up against a tree before they both melted to the forest floor.

Clothes tore. A button pinged off a tree. Her pink dress was yanked up to her waist.

"You want to be useful to me?" he growled against her neck. "Then be my nightmare. Let me see the Black Swan!"

She bit his shoulder. He groaned and shoved her deeper into the dirt.

"Say you're mine. All of you."

"I'm yours. All of me."

The trees closed in, whispering filthy encouragement. Nacht turned his back like a gentleman, though one glowing eye peeked between leaves.

Odette sank her teeth into Steffan's throat as he pressed his hard cock.

He stood and unbuttoned his white shirt and trousers.

"Get on your knees," he commanded.

She didn't hesitate. Not for a second.

She'd get on her knees in the middle of the schoolhouse, right after dismissing the children, and beg him to spank her with the ruler she uses to discipline students. All while still wearing her modest teaching dress, cheeks flushed and cunt throbbing. And she'd do it like a devoted lemming.

Bare knees pressed into the mossy ground, her thighs slick, her lips parted as the wind howled around her like it too was begging for his cock.

Before her stood the Headless Horseman.

His ghostly abdominal muscles stayed stagnant with no breath, but she didn't care. She saw the look in his bright lightning colored eyes, the storm. He was ready for her. He was ready to fuck her like nobody has ever fucked her before.

He silently commanded her to beg for that fucking.

... And being the classy French- trained woman she was she knew just how to oblige.

She reached for his cock. She could barely fit her fingers around it. It was so hard... but so cold. She stroked his length and it was as if she began to understand the life he'd stolen and the death he'd become. She didn't hesitate. Her lips wrapped around him. She sucked him with fervor, gagging on the size, tears leaking from her eyes as her throat stretched to take him. Her hands gripped his hips to steady herself, but he didn't move. He just stood, looming like a god of dick and death.

He came with no warning.

The orgasm was amazing, but unnatural. Thick ropes of hot, glowing ectoplasm shot across her face, lighting her skin with a ghostly phosphorescence. It shimmered like starlight on her skin. Dripping down her chin, her cheeks, her breasts.

The ectoplasm hissed and vanished as it touched the ground, smoke curling up from the moss as the energy of his cum dissipated.

She licked her lips and smiled, hair wild, body flushed and damp with sweat and spectral seed.

"Mets-toi à genoux," she purred.

He dropped to his knees like a statue collapsing.

No words. No need. His mouth found her pussy immediately.

She cried out unrestrained, fingers sinking into his shoulders, gripping as he devoured her like a beast starved for centuries. His tongue worked with unholy precision. licking, sucking, plunging. It felt like he was tonguing her soul. She rolled her hips against his face, grinding hard like the greedy slut she was. Her clit throbbed, her moans came in gasps, her body buckled.

She could feel the Black Swan.

She grabbed his ghostly tresses and screamed out in the most unhinged way, "Suck my clit harder, suck it like it's the best thing you've ever had the pleasure of putting your fucking filthy mouth on! Steffan...ah Steffan....STEFFAN!"

She came once, then again, and he didn't stop.
When she pushed him back, panting, her legs trembling, he looked up at her, lips glistening.

He lifted her like she weighed nothing and flipped her forward, palms against the tree, ass arched high.

Then he sheathed himself in her wet cunt. As girthy as he was there was no resistance.

And the Hollow came alive.

The trees bent. The fog screamed. Crows exploded from the branches. Her back arched and she sobbed as he fucked her with brutal, mind-shattering thrusts that knocked her forward with every slam of his hips. His hands gripped her waist, fingers biting into her skin, leaving behind a burning cold.

She could feel how hard he was. How thick. She wanted more.

He growled hips snapping harder. Her breath caught in her throat as her orgasm built. This was going to be violent.

"F-fuck," she gasped, eyes rolling back as her whole body convulsed.

Her knees buckled, her arms gave out, and she collapsed onto the ground, shaking.

Her ass jiggled with every tremor.

He noticed.

"Still trembling," he said, voice full of gravel. "You came so hard your heart stopped beating. Good girl."

She whimpered, sprawled out beneath him, his ectoplasmic cum leaking from her.

They didn't make love. They made catastrophe. Bruised knees and dirt under nails and a scream so loud it scared birds from the branches.

When it was over, Steffan was on his back panting, staring up at the sky like he'd been exorcised.

"I was never meant to be whole," he murmured. "I was meant to haunt. And I choose to haunt you."
Odette kissed him. Then she rolled to her feet, limping slightly.

Perle was gone.

"Cowardly bitch," Odette muttered.

Nacht nickered in approval.

"Well this will certainly be a walk of shame. You've destroyed my dress, Steffan."

"Good."

Together, they walked toward the bridge. One haunted. One haunter. One monster. One woman full of shadows who finally felt seen.

The Black Swan stretched her wings and smiled, because she felt seen, too.

Chapter 9

Torsion

(Twist)

The mist was different tonight.

It slithered between the roots of trees and coiled like wet smoke around Nacht's hooves as he trotted toward the old covered bridge. It clung to Odette's ankles, wrapping itself up her calves.

Her feet slapped against the damp planks, the rhythm too calm, too confident, for a woman presumed kidnapped.

The crowd was already gathered at the mouth of the bridge, torches flickering, faces pale. They had come ready for a rescue. For a fucking burning, if the ropes and pitchforks were any indication.

There was Brom. Broad-shouldered. Sweat-slick. Red-faced and raving with righteous fury. At his side was Ellis, dressed in what looked like his Sunday best, rubbing his hands together like he was praying and plotting. The crowd buzzed, confused by the image before them.
Odette stood tall, chest heaving, voice ringing out like a gunshot.

"You idiot of a man," she hissed, spittle flying. "I am not kidnapped. I am not bewitched. I am standing here…butt-ass naked…by my own deranged volition. I was going to put my clothes on once we got closer to town. The breeze feels nice."

The words hung in the air, obscene and dripping with truth.

A silence followed so complete it could have swallowed a scream. Even the creek below paused, the water was black and still.

Brom's lip twitched as his boots hit the bridge. A bell was tolling with every step.

He blinked.

"You're…" he stammered, eyes twitching down her body, to the bruises on her hips, the bite marks on her thighs. "You're fucking it."
Odette rolled her eyes so hard it was a miracle they didn't fall out of her skull.

"Wow," she deadpanned. "Stellar deduction, you backwater bag of rage issues."

That was all it took.

Brom snapped.

His twisted into a brutish, unthinking neanderthal. He whirled around to the crowd behind him, spit flying as he roared, "I'm going to kill the Horseman and this ghost-fucker, too!"

Someone gasped. A torch dropped. A child clutched her mother's skirts. Panic surged like a crack in the ice on a skating pond.

But before anyone could move...before another word could be shouted or a breath drawn...

He was already there.

Steffan.

Headless.

No sound. No warning. Just shadow, pumpkin, and steel. One moment Brom stood, chest heaving, knife in hand. The next-

SCHLUNK.

Steffan slammed a flaming jack 'o' lantern down on his head. The wet, rotted pulp of it splattered out in a spray of flame-flecked gore. It sealed to his face like molten wax, the carved mouth grinning mockingly as fire licked out from the jagged eyes. For a moment, Brom just staggered back, arms flailing. Then he let out the most unnatural, blood-curdling scream.

The first scream was a high, shrill shriek, filled with disbelief and pain. But the fire took hold. First his scalp, then his face beneath the pumpkin's smothering interior, the screams turned ragged, panicked, and primal. He clawed at the jack-o'-lantern with both hands, his fingernails tearing at the burning rind, skin sloughing from his fingers as the heat fused flesh to flame-slick gourd.

The flames ate inward, chewing down his throat, curling along his nose, and melting his ears. Smoke poured from the seams. They traveled through the grinning mouth and the triangular eyes.like some Halloween demon had come alive and taken possession of his skull. He dropped to his knees, writhing, howling, a man turned furnace.
The crowd screamed, too, some bolting, others frozen. Mothers shoved their children behind them. Old men collapsed in the dirt. No one could move fast enough. No one could help.

Inside the jack-o'-lantern, Brom's screams choked…wet, bubbling gasps that rattled through his charred throat like boiling meat. Muffled shrieks turned to throaty snarls, then to guttural, hoarse grunts, as if he were trying to cough out his own lungs. One eye burst with a pop from the heat. The smell of burning flesh, pumpkin guts, and charred hair hung in the air. It was vile.

He beat the ground with his fists, tried to rise, then collapsed sideways, twitching violently. The flames had eaten into his chest, bursting through his collar. Blisters ruptured, skin blackened and curled back to bone. Still, he lived. Still, he twitched. Still, he gargled, half-screaming, half-pleading.

That was when Steffan stepped forward.

Silent.

He raised his blade.

The sword came down in a perfect arc, and Brom's head, still engulfed in fire and the jack-o'-lantern fused to his skull, severed clean at the neck. It hit the wooden planks of the bridge with a heavy, wet thunk, the flames flaring one last time as blood jetted in a wide, arterial spray from the stump.

The body jerked once. Twice. Then collapsed in a twitching heap, smoking.

Brom's severed head rolled off the bridge and splashed into the creek. The jack-o'-lantern flickered... and died. For a moment, the only sound was torch fire crackling and the wet patter of blood dripping into the creek. Steffan remanifested his head. And placed his bloody coat over a very naked Odette.

Then he turned back towards the mob of judgmental assholes,""I would burn your homes, your fields, your precious Hollow to ash before I let one of you lay a hand on her. Odette Fournier is not your scapegoat. She is not your sinner. She is mine. And I am not a man you want for an enemy. Speak against her... and you will lose more than your pride. You'll lose your head."

The crowd trembled in horror.

Except for one...

Ellis didn't flinch. He stood still, flecked with blood, a single thick droplet trailing down his cheek. His lips twitched into something that might have been a smile, if not for his eyes.

Those eyes.

Black and bottomless. Hollow.

A grin spread across his face like it was stretched there by some invisible hand. It didn't reach those void-pits in his skull.

He looked up at Steffan.

"It's not like I haven't made sacrifices to win battles before," Ellis said.
Odette made a strangled noise. She stumbled backward, hand at her throat.

Steffan changed. No. He unleashed. His face twisted. The air around him shimmered and distorted, like heat rising from a grave. His skin cracked. Tiny glowing fractures webbed across his body, like veins of fire. Shadows retreated from him. Even Nacht, beast of the Hollow, snorted and backed away. Still not as cowardly as Perle, though.

Odette stared, trembling, hardly able to recognize the man she had clawed, kissed, begged for hours earlier.

This wasn't Steffan. This was The Headless Horseman.

He stepped forward, The crowd parted like a wound.

Some people screamed.

The preacher sobbed, hands raised to a god who clearly wasn't listening.

There was just the legend of Sleepy Hollow stalking towards the end of the bridge.

"Adderley."

Chapter 10

Le Brouillard de la Guerre

(The Fog of War)

The sound of boots in mud. That's all Brigadier General Adderley heard anymore. Marching. Drilling. Dying. The endless parade of men moving from one blood-drenched field to another.

He leaned over the table, a crude map spread before him, ink smeared from his palm. His fingers twitched. His knuckles were stained with ash and dried blood. The tent reeked of sweat, piss, and old tobacco. War was a smell that never left.

He should have been proud. He was proud. His regiment had held the ridge at Chatter's Ford. His scouts had outflanked three enemy positions near the Hudson. His men called him Iron Adderley behind his back, but he knew it. He liked it. The King of England would like it, too.

The letter had arrived just that morning, sealed in thick wax stamped with the crown's sigil. A rider brought it from New York, half-dead from the cold. Adderley took it with a grin so wide it felt like it cracked his face open. He could already hear the praise. The commendations. Perhaps even a promotion. A knighthood, if the bastard pulled his head out of his perfumed ass.

He had waited to open it until he was alone. Poured himself a glass of cheap brandy. Sat at his desk like a general.

Hands steady, he broke the seal. His eyes skimmed the first few lines with anticipation.

His brow furrowed. He read it again...and again.

Then he crumpled the paper in his fist so hard his knuckles turned white.

"Commendations to Lieutenant Steffan Weber for exemplary leadership during the skirmish at Fort Tarrytown. His actions in rallying scattered units were both courageous and decisive..."

What...what...WHAT.

Steffan Weber. That simpering, pretty-eyed fuck of a foreigner. That bastard who spoke five languages and looked like a statue carved by some bored god with too much time and too much smug. That thing with his soft smile and quiet voice who made all the tavern whores giggle like schoolgirls.

Adderley sat very still. The brandy glass shattered in his hand before he realized he was squeezing it. Blood ran in thin red lines down his wrist, but he didn't move. He just stared at the crushed parchment in his bleeding palm.

They were praising him. They were praising Steffan. Over him.

It should've ended there. But no. Steffan had to keep digging...

It was a week later. Cold wind blowing through the valley camp like it had a grudge. Men huddled around fires. Spirits were low. That night, Adderley went to a tavern. Not a proper one, just a makeshift wooden pit outside the officer's tents. He had a girl there. Cecelia. Round hips, sharp tongue, smelled like lavender and vanilla. She screamed like a fox and bit when she came. She liked him.
Until she met Steffan.

He was there, leaning against the post near the entrance. Laughing. That laugh. That smile like he wasn't at war but on holiday.

There she was, Cecelia- his Cecelia... leaning in close. Laughing back. Flipping her hair. Touching his hand.

Adderley watched them from the shadows. Fingernails digging into his palms. Breathing through his gritted teeth.

It was harmless.

But in his mind…

In his mind Steffan already had her pinned to the wall. Already had her moaning his name. Already had her legs wrapped around his waist while he fucked her like a savage.

Adderley turned and left.

He didn't sleep that night. Instead, he planned. He planned a death and that death would be a masterpiece.

White Plains would be the perfect stage. So many moving parts. So much noise. No one would notice. No one would question it.

He started planting the seeds early. He restructured his platoon. Moved Steffan to a unit that wasn't his usual. Claimed the maps required a fresh pair of eyes. He assigned him to lead a small squad of infantry…green, but eager.

Adderley chose the location personally. A low ridge with swampy grass. Trees lining the slope. Visibility was shit. Communications worse.

Adderley gave the wrong orders on purpose. Sent his own cannons the coordinates. Told them enemy units would be seen coming through the tree line just east of Steffan's position.

He practiced the lie in his head a dozen times. Fog of war. Friendly fire. A mistake. A tragedy. He would play the grieving commander. Give a stirring eulogy. Perhaps even write to the King himself.

His pulse raced thinking of it. The way the blood would look. The sound of that fine voice choked with agony. Maybe, if luck smiled on him, Steffan wouldn't die immediately.

Maybe he'd crawl on his hands and knees begging for mercy.

Adderley imagined finding him after the cannon hit. Half his face gone. One leg twisted like rope. Bleeding from the mouth. Eyes wet with betrayal. Trying to speak. Trying to understand.

Adderley would kneel and hold his hand if he had a hand left to hold.

"Such a shame," he would whisper with pity. "You almost mattered."
He laughed to himself in the dark, biting down on his knuckle to keep quiet.

The day came and it was glorious.

Smoke filled the air before the first shot was fired. The ground was already churned with mud and piss and the sick stink of death. Steffan looked alert, calm, issuing commands to his green boys like he actually gave a shit. How noble. How perfect.

Adderley watched through his spyglass from the upper ridge. He waited.

There was the signal. Three flashes.

He sent Steffan with the notice to give to the other unit. Feigning that he was the only one that could make it. The cannons roared. The earth screamed. Shells exploded around the tree line. Bodies flew. Fire bloomed.

Adderley watched the carnage.

Watched the shrapnel gut three of his men. Watched one soldier stagger away with no jaw, his teeth littering the ground.

The plan had worked. He exhaled. He raised the spyglass again. There was Steffan. Rather....what was left of him.
His body was covered in ash and blood. The cannon ball that struck him down removed his head completely.

Adderley smiled. Smiled until his face hurt.

He played the part well after. Cried on cue. Gave a rousing speech.

But at night…

At night, he dreamed that Steffan was alive. Riding his black beast with his sword drawn and a flaming pumpkin as a fucking head. Chasing him through a forest.

That dream would recur for the rest of his life and he swore one thing:

"I'll find him in the afterlife, and I'll make sure Steffan Weber never knows peace. He chased me to my death, and I will drag his soul to hell."

Chapter 11

La Ligne Entre la Justice et la Vengeance

(The Line Between Justice and Vengeance)

The bridge to Sleepy Hollow was alive with screams, death, and vengeance.

Steffan's boots struck wood as he stepped forward through the carnage. His mouth curled. His eyes gleamed. Behind him, Brom's headless body still twitched. The townspeople backed away from the crimson-slick planks, their torches now useless against the rising dark.

Adderley stood at the other end of the bridge, sword already drawn. His coat flapped like the wings of some diseased bird. His lips twisted into something close to a grin. The lines in his face carved deeper than they had any right to be. He looked like he'd already died once and liked it. Because he had.

Steffan met him step for step.

"You should have stayed dead," Adderley spat.

"You should have stayed forgotten," Steffan growled back.

Adderley raised his sword to shoulder height, and motioned toward Odette who was standing behind Steffan. His smile spread wider.

"How'd it feel," he hissed, "fucking a pussy I used to cum in so deep it still craves me? My sloppy seconds again, Steffan?"

Steffan's mouth curled into a cruel sneer.
"I never fucked that wilted crust of a bitch you called Cecelia," he said. ,"But I could have."

Adderley roared.

Their swords met like crashing thunder. Metal screamed. Sparks flew. The bridge shook under the weight of their hatred. Adderley struck low then high then side then again and again and again. Steffan parried with one hand and with the other reached behind his back.

Fire rose from his palm. Jack o'lanterns flared to life in midair. The carved faces snarled with twisted teeth and wild eyes. He hurled them with furious precision.

Adderley dodged one. Then another.

The third missed him and exploded into a mass of shrieking flame that ripped into the crowd.

A man's head flew from his shoulders and spun in the air like a grotesque coin toss. A woman screamed as fire melted half her face. Another woman's cry was cut short by the sickening sound of a skull splitting open. The crowd scattered in a frenzy. Wailing. Scrambling. Slipping in the blood.

Steffan saw it but didn't stop. Justice doesn't pause.

Adderley laughed.

"That's not justice" he spat. "That's just murder with a prettier name."

Steffan bared his teeth.

"You don't know justice," he growled. "You hunted me when I trusted you. You killed to silence your own insecurities!"

Adderley lunged again. His blade caught Steffan across the cheek. Ectoplasm poured down in a hot gush. Steffan spun and answered with his own blade, slicing Adderley across the chest so deep you could see the white beneath the red.

"Justice" Adderley hissed. "is vengeance with a hero complex."

Their swords locked at the hilts. Faces inches apart. Sweat and ectoplasm and spit mixing on their skin.

"There's a difference," Steffan snarled.

"What difference?" Adderley said.

"Justice makes the world habitable," Steffan growled. "Vengeance makes it burn."

"Then I'm the fucking lit match," Adderley snapped.

Behind them the crowd had mostly fled. Only the unlucky and the paralyzed remained. But one figure forced her way forward. Screaming. Crying.

Michelle.

The gypsy pushed through the fleeing crowd. Her eyes were wild. Her pendant glowed like emerald fire. So bright it looked like it was burning through her skin.

"Odette," she screamed. "Odette, you have to run. You have to make it back. You don't understand. You don't understand what you're standing in."

Her voice cracked.

"They're not fighting like men anymore. They've tapped The Hollow's fury. It's going to consume them and it's going to take you, too!"

Odette staggered forward. Blood slick between her thighs. Her breath ragged. She looked down at the creek. The water below the bridge was too cold to swim across.

She looked at the woods behind her. No cover. No time.

She had to run now or never.

Michelle's hand stretched toward her.

"Please" she begged. "You have to come to me. Now."

Steffan and Adderley moved to the right side of the bridge in their fury. Odette saw the path. Saw her way across.

She dropped Steffan's coat and ran.

Heart thundering. Legs shaking. Tits bouncing. Every part of her screamed with pain and cold and terror.

She passed between them.

But Adderley's blade didn't know she wasn't part of the fight. It swung wide.

It caught her across the throat. Not clean. Not shallow. The edge carved through her skin. Through her veins. Through her windpipe.

Odette stopped moving. Her mouth opened. No sound. Only blood. It spilled from her mouth. Her nose. Her neck. A spray of red painted the bridge. Her final signature.

She dropped to her knees.

Her eyes turned from cerulean to ink. No light. No warmth. Just bottomless black.

She stared ahead..straight through Michelle.

And with a wet choking cough she whispered,
"Oui... Maîtresse..."

Then she pitched forward face first onto the wood. Blood pooled around her like a halo.

Steffan didn't turn. Adderley didn't flinch.

Michelle's hands flew to her pendant, the glowing green light now pulsing so violently it was like watching a dying star implode. Her fingers bled from clutching it too tight.

Sleepy Hollow went silent.

A violent shudder exploded beneath their feet. The wood groaned and cracked like it might tear in half. The creek below raged, white froth foaming around the rocks as though it too felt the death of something sacred. Trees bowed at their trunks. Leaves spiraled upward instead of down.

Steffan dropped to his knees. It wasn't grief. Not yet. It was shock. Then rage.

The Horseman screamed.

The fiery crack down his neck flared with light so intense it turned white. His body glowed from the inside out.

He looked at Odette's corpse. Then he looked at Adderley.

He threw his sword down. No steel now.

He lunged with his bare hands.
He tackled Adderley with a force that split the railing of the bridge. Boards cracked and groaned beneath them. They rolled across blood, across flame, across death. Fists flying. Teeth bared. Steffan bit Adderley's shoulder so hard he felt a tendon snap between his jaws.

Adderley headbutted him. Drove his thumb toward Steffan's eye. Tried to dig it out. Steffan shrieked and clawed his face open, tearing down across his cheek and dragging skin with it.

"You killed her!"

Steffan's voice was ragged, demonic.

"You brought her here," Adderley hissed. "You made her a target. Odette died because of you!"

Steffan slammed his fist into Adderley's jaw again and again until the bone crunched and his fingers were slick with ectoplasm and teeth.

"You don't get to say her name."

His fingers wrapped around Adderley's throat. He began to squeeze.

Behind them, the bridge groaned louder. The air above them shimmered. Specters began to emerge from the creek. Pale faces. Hollow eyes. The spirits of the Hollow watching. Pulled from their resting place.

Michelle began to chant.

She raised both hands to the sky. The pendant exploded with green light that shot upward into a pillar and then outward like a shockwave. It shoved the spirits back, at least for a breath.

"Stop," she screamed. "This will end you both. She's gone. She's gone and if you kill each other now, you'll never leave. You'll become what you hate. You'll become them."

Adderley twisted beneath Steffan and laughed.

"That's the point."

Steffan stood.

The fire in his chest was blinding. The rage in his gut incandescent. Odette's blood still steamed where it touched his boots.

"You want vengeance," he said. "Then you can have mine."

Steffan raised both hands, palms glowing white-hot from within. The air cracked. The sky darkened. Every jack-o'-lantern in the air widened their grin as if they understood.

They descended.

Flames erupted from their gaping mouths as they collided with the bridge, igniting the wood in jagged streaks of gold fire. The boards screamed beneath the weight of flame, splitting down the center as smoke surged into the sky like the Hollow itself was vomiting out the sun.

Adderley was trapped.

The fire curled around him like a noose. His blade dropped. His grin, still in place, twisted higher as the heat began to peel the skin from his face.

He laughed. Laughed even as the flames rose higher. Laughed as the bridge beneath him blackened and buckled.

But then the laughter cracked.

Then it choked.
Then it screamed.

It was the scream of a soul being peeled apart layer by layer. The scream of a man who thought vengeance was power, only to realize it was his damnation. His flesh melted. His eyes boiled. His soul, tethered too long to rot and hate, shredded into ribbons of light and vanished from the universe with one final, strangled cry.

He let his vengeance be his undoing. Sleepy Hollow swallowed him whole.

Adderley stood laughing as the bridge vanished into hellfire.

Chapter 12

Encore un Fantôme

(One More Ghost)

Steffan stood on the bridge.

The fires had died, but the scent of ash clung to the air. Smoke rose from the blackened wood in spirals, rising toward a sky that couldn't decide if it was night or morning. The sun had not yet dared to rise over Sleepy Hollow. The creek bubbled beneath the bridge.

He hadn't moved.

The weight of what he'd failed to do pinned him on an iron cross. His hands, once balled into fists of fire, now hung useless at his sides. The jack o'lanterns were gone. The spirits had gone quiet. The Hollow had gone still.

All except for the corpse behind him.

Odette.

Lying face-down where she fell. Her blood had dried in thick black smears around her, her hair tangled in the broken boards, mouth slightly parted as if she was still in the middle of a word she didn't get to finish. A strange peace had settled over her, but it was not the kind of peace that followed salvation. It was the peace of something unresolved. Like a page ripped from a book.

Michelle stepped onto the bridge. Her boots made no sound. She looked like a ghost herself. The green pendant at her neck pulsed faintly with dying light. She took a single step toward Odette.

Steffan turned his head and looked at her. He didn't speak, but she felt it…his warning. His sorrow. His fury. A psychic scream made entirely of silence. She stopped moving.

Her voice was barely above a whisper.

"My soul is done with this place," she said. "I have no friends. I have no family. I travel. My pendant…" her fingers brushed it "…keeps me here. Attaches my soul to my vessel. To this Earth. But maybe…"

She stepped forward again.

" I cannot save her vessel, but maybe I can save her soul."
Steffan's glowing eyes didn't blink. Didn't soften. Just watched.

Michelle knelt beside Odette's broken body. She reached out and brushed the hair gently from her face.

"Steffan," she said, "you ran under the assumption that killing Adderley would free you. That vengeance would break the curse. But here you are. Still standing. Still haunting Sleepy Hollow."

He said nothing.

She glanced at the dried blood across Odette's throat.

"Love is unfinished business," she said.

Her hands moved with practiced slowness. She reached behind her neck and unclasped the pendant. The chain hissed as it came free, the gem glowing brighter now, as if sensing what was coming.

Michelle's hands trembled as she lowered it to Odette's throat. The wound had clotted black, the skin around it purple. The moment the green crystal touched her, it flared.

Michelle smiled.

"Enjoy this chapter," she said to Steffan.

Then she stood and turned to the east as the sun began to rise over Sleepy Hollow.

She didn't look back as she burned out.

∞ ∞ ∞

The funerals happened in mass. No one mentioned ghosts. No one dared say the word "curse." People from across the Hudson Valley came with casseroles and candles and arms full of sympathy. They mourned the bystanders who died in what the papers called "a devastating bridge fire." It was a lie, of course, but a convenient one.

The fire made for an easy scapegoat.

Even the bridge was gone. All that remained was scorched stone and the smell of soaked ash. They said lightning hit it. They said dry wood sparked. They said someone dropped a lantern. They said anything but the truth.

They buried them all. All except Odette.

They said the flames must have taken her. That the wind carried her body into the creek and away. No bones. No ash.

Then... the sightings began. They came from children first.

The little ones said they saw Ms. Fournier dancing in the woods. A woman with long blonde hair and glowing eyes, who wore a beautiful blue dress that fluttered behind her. She didn't speak. She didn't walk. She floated.

The parents didn't believe them. Until the dreams started. Until the townsfolk began waking up in the middle of the night with the sound of footsteps on their roofs and soft humming outside their windows.

The sheriff saw her in the trees. He followed her out past the old church and never returned. A hunter saw her kneeling beside the creek. When he blinked, she was gone.

Her memory never had a resting place. She was never buried and never had a coffin.

Steffan stayed.

Remaining the Headless Horseman. Remaining a legend. He haunted the charred remains of the bridge, sometimes crouching at the edge like a gargoyle, sometimes vanishing into the fog. But he always came back.

He never spoke.

Not until the night he heard humming.

He stood up slowly. His eyes glowed faintly as they scanned the mist.

The humming got louder.

He stepped toward the sound. There she was.

Odette.

Her skin was pale, nearly luminous. Her throat was healed, but the scar still pulsed faintly green. The pendant Michelle gave her hung tight against her skin, now fused with her body like a second heart. Her eyes, no longer cerulean, no longer black. They had become a spectral blue that glowed even when she blinked.

She didn't speak. She just looked at him and smiled. Then she turned and walked into the trees.

Steffan took Nacht's reins and followed.

Some nights, if you walk far enough into the Hollow, you can still see them. A figure in a blue dress, glowing in the moonlight. Behind her, rides the Headless Horseman. Haunting the forest...together.

Michelle's soul, untethered, dissolved into the ley lines of the Earth, and some claim she still walks between dimensions, dragging the veil open with her fingers and slipping through cracks in the sky. Wherever she is, she never took her pendant back.

She gave it away. Gave Odette a second ending. A new chapter.

Sleepy Hollow has one more ghost.

Epilogue

Lègendes

(Legends)

The smell of sugar and browned butter danced through the little kitchen filling the air with comfort.

A young woman stood barefoot on the tile floor, placing the last perfect madeleine into a small ivory box tied with red ribbon. They were golden, shell-shaped, lightly crisped on the edge, dusted in powdered sugar. She smiled down at them with pride, brushing flour from her cheek with the back of her wrist.

Her black hair was twisted into a high, tight bun. Her new navy-blue headmistress uniform hugged her figure in all the right places. She didn't need to look in the mirror. She felt radiant.

Today was her first day. Her first day as Headmistress of the Sleepy Hollow Schoolhouse.

"Mother, I'm off!" she called as she grabbed her coat and the dessert box.

Her mother's voice floated down from upstairs. "Tempest, I know you'll do great!"

She grinned. Her boots clicked confidently down the hall as she left the house. No headmaster or mistress had lived in the old schoolhouse for years. They all stayed off-site now. Safer that way, people said.

She didn't care.

Tempest liked old things. She liked strange places. She liked Sleepy Hollow.

The walk was brisk. The schoolhouse stood at the end of a gravel path, slate-roofed and half-swallowed by trees. Ivy climbed its sides. A brass bell hung above the door, still tarnished from storms older than she was.

She opened the door and marched in. She was always a confident, bad bitch.

The children were already seated, their eyes wide and curious. Something about the place felt sacred.

"Hello, students," she said with her warmest smile. "I brought you something."
She placed the dessert box on her desk and opened it with a little flourish. The madeleines gleamed.

"I made these by hand," she said. "They're a tribute to a former headmistress here. She was a friend of my mother's. I hope you'll enjoy this little piece of French culture."

The children cheered quietly and whispered to each other. One of them reached for a cookie and whispered, "Merci…"

Tempest's smile deepened. She turned to glance out the window and could swear she saw a shadow flicker through the trees. Then it disappeared. Tempest turned back towards the children and started her introductory lessons.

Odette tilted her head and smiled softly. She always watched over the children of Sleepy Hollow. She would never let harm touch them. They deserved a chance. Because war had broken everything and they were the only hope left.

Odette turned away from the schoolhouse.

Steffan was leaning against a tree behind her, arms crossed, his long coat fluttering faintly in the breeze. Nacht stood beside him, snorting gently, eyes glowing.

"Do you see her?" she asked.

"I see her," he said.

"She's a product of Brom," Odette whispered, "but she's also a child of Katrina."

Steffan raised an eyebrow.

"Katrina was kind to me. Always."

"Sounds like someone's getting sentimental," Steffan murmured.

"Haven't you ever heard," she said, "that the daughter shouldn't pay for the sins of the father?"

Steffan smirked. "No. But I have heard that ghosts who talk too much need to be silenced in other ways."

"Oh?" Odette purred. "Are you going to lecture me, Horseman?"

"I could," he said, voice gravel-rich. "But I'm better with my hands."

She stepped closer. Her fingers brushed his coat. "Still thinking with your sword, I see."

"You make it hard to think with anything else."

"Then stop thinking."

She kissed him, hard.

Her hands yanked his coat open and shoved it off his shoulders. His mouth collided with hers. His fingers sank into her hair, tugging it loose, letting it spill down her back. Her legs wrapped around his waist. He pressed her against the nearest tree

.

They were ghosts.

They had no blood, but they burned with a primal, horny flame. They had no hearts, but when they fucked, skin slapped like war drums.

It's like the whole Hollow's cunt was wet.

She clawed at his chest and he tore her dress apart. Threads unraveled midair, vanishing into mist. His coat fell in pieces at his feet. .

His mouth found her neck, her jaw, her nipples.

"Suck harder," she hissed.

He sucked both of her nipples until they were puffy and purple. Then he grabbed her tits hard and ran his thumbs over the tops of them. She moaned softly.

He ran his tongue down her abdomen and stopped at her belly button placing a kiss, just there. Odette shuttered.
He moved lower and lower and lower. And lightly trailed his tongue along her wet slit so she could barely feel it. He knew what he was doing. He was leaving her wanting more. He wanted her to beg. After all this time, he still always wanted her to beg.

His lightning colored eyes met her beautiful blue ones as he looked up at her. His mouth was close enough to her cunt where she could feel his cool breath on her clit.

"Please…" she wined.

"Please what?" Asked Steffan smugly.

"Please use your mouth on my clit…" She said with more desperation.

"Who are you giving me today?" he asked her.

"Who do you want?" She panted.

"All of you. Give me the whore that the Black Swan is. Give me the lover that the White Swan is."

Her eyes darkened, "Suck my fucking clit."

"Oui, maîtresse."

And with that his mouth engulfed her clit entirely and with no mercy. Sucking, nibbling,and swirling his tongue over and over and over again. She threw her head back and moaned loudly…eyes wide looking up at a heaven that would never accept her. But that's okay, because getting her pussy eaten out by the Headless Horseman was a religous experience.

He moved lower, sliding his tongue inside her cunt, tasting every bit of her. He pressed his tongue upward, making her clit throb.

He felt that. He snaked his arm under her thigh and tell his hand to reach the top of her pussy. He rolled her swollen clit in-between his index finger and thumb. Her mouth dropped open and she grabbed his hair.

She could feel her orgasm building in the pit of her
stomach. But she didn't want to cum on his tongue
today.
She pulled his head back from her wet pussy and he
crawled up her body, smashing his glistening lips
against hers.

She tasted so sweet today. Like crème brûlée.
They broke the kiss... panting. He had a questioning
look in his eyes that she knew all too well...

He wanted a command.

"Fuck me ..."

He unbuttoned his trousers and pulled out his thick,
hard cock. This was not only a representation of his lust
for her but of his obsession. She wanted to be fucked?
He was going give her the best fuck she's ever had in her
whole life...or death.

He stood, pulling her on her feet with him and turned
her toward the tree.

"Bend over and spread your legs, Maitresse."

She parted her legs and could feel the cool breeze on
her dripping cunt. But not for long. He slammed into her
with such force the tree groaned. Her head snapped
back. She cried out. His hands dug into her thighs
spreading them wider.

The forest watched.

The Hollow listened.

And Steffan made her scream like she was being murdered all over again.

"Say it," he growled into her ear.

"Say what?" she whimpered.

"Say you're mine."

"I'm yours," she moaned.

"Louder!"

He thrusted into her harder so the reverb from the slam rippled up her ass.

"I'M YOURS , I'm yours, I'm.. AH AH AH AH-"

Her orgasm ripped through her and her walls clenched around the girth of his cock. She collapsed in his arms. He buried his face in her shoulder and came with a growl that shook the trees.

They collapsed together in the grass. The green light of her pendant glowed against his chest.

"I love you."

"I love you, too."

Steffan Weber and Odette Fournier are not ghosts. They are the legends of Sleepy Hollow.

They are its scream in the silence. Its shadow on the road. The last kiss of fog before dawn.

You might feel them watching. You might hear laughter where there should be none. You might swear the trees are breathing.

They will never rest.

And when the ivy on the schoolhouse walls shiver without wind…

When the forest leans too close to town…

That's when you know:
Odette and the Headless Horseman are riding.

(The End)

Recipes from the Book

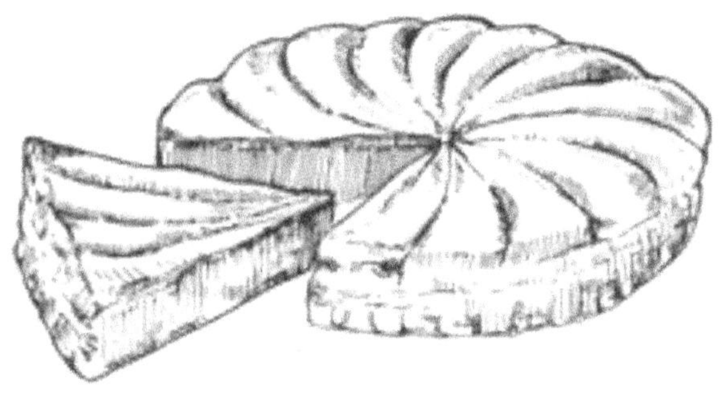

Odette's Gâteau de Riz

(French Rice Pudding Cake)

Silky custard, caramel, and rice baked into nostalgic perfection.

Ingredients:

For the caramel:

* ½ cup (100g) granulated sugar
* 2 tablespoons water

For the rice pudding:

* 1 cup (200g) short-grain rice (arborio or round rice)
* 4 cups (1 liter) whole milk
* 1 vanilla bean (or 1½ tsp vanilla extract)
* ⅓ cup (70g) sugar
* Pinch of salt
* 2 eggs
* 1 tablespoon butter (for greasing)

Instructions:

1. Make the caramel
   In a saucepan, combine sugar and water. Heat over medium without stirring until the mixture turns golden amber. Immediately pour it into a buttered loaf pan or round cake mold. Swirl to coat the bottom evenly.

2. Make the rice pudding
   Rinse the rice under cold water. In a separate saucepan, bring milk to a simmer with the split vanilla bean and a pinch of salt. Add rice and cook gently,

stirring often, until tender and thick (about 30–40 minutes). Remove the vanilla bean pod.

3. Sweeten & bind

Stir in sugar. Let the rice cool slightly (so it doesn't scramble the eggs), then whisk in the beaten eggs.

4. Bake

Preheat oven to 350°F (175°C). Pour the rice mixture over the caramel in the mold. Bake for 35–40 minutes or until just set and golden on top.

5. Cool & unmold

Let cool slightly before turning out onto a plate. Chill before serving to allow the caramel to soak in.

Tempest's Madeleines

Delicate shell-shaped sponge cakes with a buttery lemon kick.

Ingredients (Makes ~24):

* ½ cup (115g) unsalted butter, melted and cooled
* 2 large eggs
* ½ cup (100g) sugar
* 1 tsp vanilla extract
* Zest of 1 lemon (optional: or use orange zest)
* 1 cup (120g) all-purpose flour
* 1 tsp baking powder
* Pinch of salt
* Powdered sugar for dusting
* Butter + flour for greasing the madeleine pan

Instructions:

1. Prepare the pan
   Generously grease your madeleine mold with melted butter and dust with flour. Chill in the fridge.

2. Make the batter
   Beat eggs and sugar with an electric mixer until thick and pale (about 5 minutes). Add vanilla and lemon zest.

3. Add dry ingredients
   Sift together flour, baking powder, and salt. Fold into the egg mixture gently.

4. Incorporate butter
   Gently fold in the cooled melted butter in three additions until smooth. Cover and chill the batter for at

least 1 hour (up to overnight). This helps the classic "bump" form.

5. Bake

Preheat oven to 375°F (190°C). Spoon 1 tablespoon of batter into each mold (don't spread it). Bake 8–10 minutes until puffed and golden.

6. Cool & dust

Let cool a few minutes, then gently remove from pan. Dust with powdered sugar before serving.

Flame in the Hollow Inspired Cocktails

Blood on the Bridge

A smoky, crimson cocktail that burns like vengeance and finishes like ash.

Base Spirit: Bourbon
Ingredients:
2 oz bourbon

½ oz cherry liqueur

½ oz lemon juice

¼ oz maple syrup

Dash of bitters

Black lava salt or smoked salt rim (optional)

Brandied cherry garnish

Instructions:
Shake with ice. Strain into a rocks glass over a large cube. Garnish with a cherry. Sip slow…vengeance lingers.

Nacht's Gallop

A dark, velvety drink that hits like hooves at full speed.

Base Spirit: Spiced Rum
Ingredients:
2 oz spiced rum (or black rum for extra depth)

1 oz coffee liqueur (like Kahlúa)

1 oz cold brew concentrate

½ oz vanilla syrup or Demerara syrup

Heavy cream float (optional, for a ghostly swirl)

Crushed espresso bean or shaved dark chocolate for garnish

Instructions:
Shake rum, liqueur, cold brew, and syrup with ice.
Strain into a rocks glass over fresh ice. Float cream on top if desired. Garnish with chocolate or espresso dust. Drink when the wind howls.

Ride at Midnight

Bubbly and eerie like a haunted orchard.

Ingredients:

½ oz absinthe

¾ oz elderflower liqueur

½ oz apple juice

Top with chilled prosecco or brut sparkling wine

Thin apple slice or dried blood orange wheel for garnish

Instructions:
Shake absinthe, elderflower, and apple juice with ice.
Strain into a flute or coupe glass and top with prosecco.
Garnish with something that feels like it came from the
woods.

Acknowledgments

To my amazing Street Team:

Bea Barros

Kirby

Lilly Hernandez

My Favorite Bitch Angela

Ophelia Paine

@badash.bookclub

@red.angel.reviews

@whimsical.bookie

Thank you for being there for me through the entire writing process. For promoting me, for showing up, and for giving me the strength to keep going even when I wanted to stop. You're my biggest cheerleaders and I'm forever grateful for each of you. This book wouldn't exist without your love and loud support.

To my family. Thank you for pushing me to finally sit down and write this story. For giving me the time and space to do it, even when I had a hundred other things going on. Thank you for always supporting me and my ever-growing list of strange collections, especially the Headless Horseman statues, and for never once asking me to tone down the weird. Being myself has always felt easy because of you.

And a special shout out to Nick Burns. Without you, none of these characters would know how to insult anyone properly. Your creative genius in the art of smartassery is unmatched and deeply appreciated.

Thank you for riding into the Hollow with me. I'll see you at midnight.

www.ingramcontent.com/pod-product-compliance
Lightning Source LLC
Chambersburg PA
CBHW071327140726
47996CB00005B/1863